Parenting

Preparing Adolescents for
Responsible Adulthood

*(Dbt Skills to Help Your Teen Navigate Emotional
and Behavioral Challenges)*

David Bridges

Published By **Jordan Levy**

David Bridges

All Rights Reserved

Parenting: Preparing Adolescents for Responsible Adulthood (Dbt Skills to Help Your Teen Navigate Emotional and Behavioral Challenges)

ISBN 978-1-7771996-5-4

No part of this guidebook shall be reproduced in any form without permission in writing from the publisher except in the case of brief quotations embodied in critical articles or reviews.

Legal & Disclaimer

The information contained in this book is not designed to replace or take the place of any form of medicine or professional medical advice. The information in this book has been provided for educational & entertainment purposes only.

The information contained in this book has been compiled from sources deemed reliable, and it is accurate to the best of the Author's knowledge; however, the Author cannot guarantee its accuracy and validity and cannot be held liable for any errors or omissions. Changes are periodically made to this book. You must consult your doctor or get professional medical advice before using any of the suggested remedies, techniques, or information in this book.

Upon using the information contained in this book, you agree to hold harmless the Author from and against any damages, costs, and expenses, including any legal fees potentially resulting from the application of any of the information provided by this guide. This disclaimer applies to any damages or injury caused by the use and application, whether directly or indirectly, of any advice or information presented, whether for breach of contract, tort, negligence, personal injury, criminal intent, or under any other cause of action.

You agree to accept all risks of using the information presented inside this book. You need to consult a professional medical practitioner in order to ensure you are both able and healthy enough to participate in this program.

Table Of Contents

Chapter 1: Building A Supportive Environment 1

Chapter 2: Promoting A Positive Mindset 13

Chapter 3: Developing Social Skills 23

Chapter 4: Managing Symptoms And Behavior.. 32

Chapter 5: Implementing Behavioral Strategies.. 42

Chapter 6: Addressing School Challenges 51

Chapter 7: Navigating Life Transitions.... 60

Chapter 8: Transitioning To College And Adulthood... 74

Chapter 9: Understanding Stubborn Children 84

Chapter 10: Parenting A Strong-Willed Child.. 92

Chapter 11: Dealing With Aggressive, Defiant And Disobedient Children........ 115

Chapter 12: Parenting Skills 132

Chapter 13: Child Care 146

Chapter 14: Imparting Moral Education To Kids 155

Chapter 15: Definition Of Positive Parenting 164

Chapter 16: Common Behavioral Challenges In Each Stage...................... 173

Chapter 1: Building A Supportive Environment

Creating a Structured Home Environment

Your daughter's ADHD goals will benefit from having a installed home surroundings, which can also beneficial useful useful resource in her dependancy formation and upkeep. She could be better capable of control her time, keep organized, and stay focused in a primarily based domestic setting. She becomes extra self enough and self-disciplined as a end end result.

Establishing a everyday time table is step one in giving your daughter a regulated domestic surroundings. This time table want to encompass everyday sports at the aspect of getting up on the equal time every day, going to mattress on the identical time every night, and eating everyday meals on the equal instances. Regular bodily interest must moreover be covered, which includes every day walks or one of a type types of exercise. Your toddler will enjoy greater regular and be higher able to control her time if she follows a time desk that never adjustments.

Setting easy expectations and limitations is the second level in supplying your daughter with a controlled home environment. Ensure that she is privy to what is expected of her in addition to the repercussions of breaking the pointers. It is likewise important to provide her exceptional reinforcement whilst she respects the regulations and to be regular with punishment. She will research energy of thoughts and that her actions have repercussions due to this.

The next degree in giving your daughter a regulated domestic environment is to provide her sufficient property. This consists of making sure that she has all the device she desires for each her pursuits and her studies. Having an entire lot of books and other belongings available to her can even help her have a look at and preserve prepared. Giving her get right of get admission to to to those device will useful resource in her ability to interest and expand.

Establishing a quiet and serene atmosphere is the fourth level in giving your daughter a controlled home environment. Distractions like video video video games, television, and one of a kind technology want to be eliminated so that you can accumulate this. Also, it's miles crucial to hold the residence litter-free and to reduce noise stages. She will pay interest and stay on challenge with the beneficial resource of this.

To provide your daughter a dependent domestic surroundings, provide her not unusual breaks and incentives. This is the 6th segment. She may be higher capable of pay attention and stay on the proper tune if she takes normal breaks. Incentives will offer her the motivation to preserve on path and to stay prepared.

Ultimately, it's miles crucial to exercising consistency and staying strength. It will take time to installation a everyday and provide her the sources she dreams, so it's miles important to be chronic and affected person. She could be better organized to address her ADHD after she has normal a recurring and can manipulate her time extra skillfully.

Establishing a regulated domestic environment on your daughter is a crucial detail of parenting. She will studies power of will, a way to hold prepared, and a manner to stay on the right music. It is crucial to assemble a each day schedule, set clean expectancies and obstacles, deliver her with appropriate belongings, create a quiet and serene environment, and provide her with not unusual pauses and incentives. Your daughter will studies the competencies she desires to higher manage her ADHD in case you are affected person and continual together along with her.

Establishing sporting events and schedules

Creating exercises and timetables to your ADHD teen is vital to supporting her manipulate her signs and symptoms and symptoms and attain achievement. Lack of shape also can make it hard for children with ADHD to organise and recognition on chores, so retaining them heading in the right direction requires preserving a everyday ordinary and timetable. Making a time desk for your daughter may additionally want to experience intimidating, however it would not want to be. Here are a few guidelines for developing timetables and sporting activities in your daughter with ADHD:

1. Create a ordinary bedtime and wake-up time: By doing this, you may make sure that your daughter gets enough sleep and is ready for the day earlier. She can be better capable of listen and continue to be aware all through the day if she has a regular bedtime and wake-up time.

2. Establish everyday mealtimes: It's essential for youngsters with ADHD to devour meals at regular intervals inside the direction of the day because it allows to control their blood sugar stages and offers them electricity. Your daughter might be capable of live on time table and prevent feeling like she is constantly gambling "entice-up" together together with her food if she eats on the identical time each day.

3. Create a homework recurring: Your daughter desires a everyday homework time desk to be prepared and committed to her instructors. She can be much more likely to stay on mission and cease her duties on time if she develops a

recurring that includes hooked up instances for starting and completing her schoolwork.

four. Include exercise: Exercise is useful for children with ADHD because it improves interest and lets in to lower stress. She can also moreover preserve active and preserve interest on her sports via which includes some kind of exercising in her each day normal, which include a walk or motorcycle ride.

5. Plan amusement time: It's critical to make certain your daughter has time for amusing pursuits like analyzing or gambling video video games. After an prolonged day of targeting her paintings, she may be capable of unwind and relaxation way to this.

6. Make circle of relatives time a subject: Children with ADHD benefit from spending time with their families. A exceptional approach to bond together with your daughter and make her sense cherished and supported is to have circle of relatives food or sport evenings.

To help your daughter with ADHD manage her symptoms and be triumphant, you want to set up a everyday and timetable for her. At first, it could seem a bit overwhelming, however with the right techniques, you may installation a regular on the way to preserve your daughter prepared and centered on her obligations. When she receives used to her new dependancy and agenda, keep in mind to be patient and information even as also displaying her pretty some love and assist.

Establishing Limitations and Penalties

Setting limits and punishments for your daughter's conduct might be tough on the same time as she has ADHD, as a discern. Yet, it's miles a essential component of parenting and can train your daughter a way to manipulate her behaviour and make wiser alternatives.

For your daughter with ADHD, it is important to establish easy barriers so she knows what is predicted of her. These rules need to be related to effective actions and be age-suitable. You can also installation a rule that announces, for instance, that during case your daughter would possibly now not do her obligations with the useful resource of a specific time every day, she will be able to go through the consequences.

Maintaining obstacles after they had been hooked up is vital. While it might be hard, doing that is essential in case you want to train your daughter that the subjects she does have repercussions. Giving in and absolving her of duty ought to absolutely train her that her movements are perfect.

Consistent with the conduct, punishments should be proportionate to it. An example of a effect is probably dropping a privilege, like watching TV or playing video video video games, if your daughter is not doing her duties. If your daughter is not doing her responsibilities, the penalty have to be more extreme than if she became simply being disruptive. The punishment ought to be commensurate with the conduct.

It's essential to permit your teen recognise why her actions have repercussions. She has a better understanding of why she is being punished and the charge of abiding with the resource of the hints as a end result. This is also a super time to talk to her approximately how she will be able to change her conduct.

Positive reinforcement need to get hold of similarly to establishing limits and punishments. Praise your daughter for adhering to the recommendations and for making smart picks to obtain this. This teaches her that making the high-quality choices is essential and that she can be rewarded for her actions.

Setting limits and punishments to your daughter who has ADHD is probably hard regular. Yet, it is a important detail of parenting and may teach your daughter the manner to manipulate her behaviour and make wiser selections. Your daughter may additionally hold near why her movements have repercussions and how she will be able to work on changing them if you set clear limits and outcomes, adhere to them, and provide excellent reinforcement.

Organizing the residence to reduce distractions

It might be difficult to organise the house to restrict distractions when you have an

Attention Deficit Hyperactivity Disorder (ADHD) kid. It's important to offer a placing for you to resource your daughter in keeping organisation and interest.

Decluttering is the first step in arranging the house to reduce distractions to your daughter with ADHD. The residence should be smooth of the whole thing that is useless or no longer in use due to the fact clutter may be quite distracting. Toys, clothing, literature, and extraordinary distracting devices fall under this magnificence. In order to make subjects easy to discover whilst required, it is also important to ensure that the entirety has a devoted place.

Making a completely unique place of work on your daughter is the following step. There have to be a place in which she will be able to effects pay attention without being distracted. This may be a desk or computer in her room or a gap inside the dwelling region. Ensure that the vicinity is comfortable and that each one required objects are there.

The 0.33 step is to set up a every day time desk. This ought to embody precise time for schoolwork, studying, and extracurricular sports activities out of doors. Your daughter can be able to hold organized and focused with this. Also, it's important to ensure that your daughter observes everyday mealtimes, bedtimes, and wake up hours. Her body clock can be more regulated as a cease result, which might also moreover assist her live targeted and green.

Reduce distractions because the fourth motion. Turning off the tv, video video games, and different technological gadgets falls below this class. Also, it's far essential to hold visitor numbers under test because of the fact they might be very stressful. In order to enhance recognition, it's also important to hold the noise diploma within the home to a minimum. Reduce out of doors noise as an awful lot as you can, if in any respect viable.

The fifth step is to provide your daughter the organizing resources she needs. This consists of a calendar, notepads, submitting cabinets, and different gear for organizing that would help her in prioritising her duties and coping with her time. Also, it's far critical to ensure your teen knows in which to locate these things and that they may be every to be had to her.

The advent of a praise system is the 6th segment. Your daughter can be stimulated through way of this to preserve her organisation and interest. Incentives should likely range from more time spent wearing out a desired hobby to a deal with or specific enjoy. Consistency with incentives is crucial considering it'll encourage the favored behaviour.

You can help your daughter pay interest and preserve organized through doing the actions listed above to set up a beneficial surroundings. She can be capable of maximise her time and power and reduce distractions as a cease end result. Keeping in mind that company enterprise is a manner and that it takes time to increase is likewise vital. You could make your daughter's residence orderly and freed from distractions in case you are chronic and affected individual.

Chapter 2: Promoting A Positive Mindset

Encouraging vanity and self assurance

It can be difficult and notable to elevate a kid with hobby deficit hyperactivity illness (ADHD). Because of the problems they encounter in their research, interpersonal interactions, and exclusive endeavours, women with ADHD once in a while battle with horrible shallowness and lack of self assure.

As a stop result, it is important for parents and exceptional adults to guide ADHD girls in growing their experience of self confidence and self perception.

Providing help and knowledge is one of the most essential sports activities even as selling arrogance and self warranty in ADHD ladies. It's crucial to understand the problems the lady is having and to be present to take note of her at the same time as she desires it. She wants to be reminded of her abilties and assisted in coming across new programs for them. It is also beneficial to offer her reward even as she succeeds considering this may encourage her to don't forget in her competencies.

Setting possible goals with ADHD girls is an additional critical step in helping them boom their conceitedness and self warranty. This includes putting in worrying but viable goals. It's essential to encourage the female to go in the direction of her dreams, even though they appear too tough. When she succeeds, it'll growth her self-warranty and help her experience extra capable. In addition, it's far critical to make sure the objectives are possible and do no longer grow to be too formidable.

Providing the female with admirable role models is also crucial. This may be executed thru having her examine approximately successful ladies with ADHD or by way of way of way of revealing her to one of a type a success women with ADHD. This can also moreover assist her in for the purpose that, regardless of her ADHD, she is able to conducting her dreams and succeeding.

Ultimately, it is essential to provide an environment in which the lady feels free to percentage her thoughts and emotions. It is crucial that she enjoy free to share her reports and that she gets no complaint. It's essential to assist her in developing coping mechanisms for her ADHD and for coping with her emotions. This may be finished via way of teaching her healthful coping mechanisms like deep respiratory, mindfulness, and galvanizing self-communicate.

Parents and unique adults who take care of ADHD girls may promote conceitedness and self perception with the resource of using the ones strategies. It's essential to expose her manual and records, help her in making realistic goals, offer her remarkable function models, and offer a stable surroundings wherein she might also air her feelings. In this way, mother and father and unique adults can also aid their daughter's improvement of a robust revel in of self-worth and self-self guarantee.

Helping ladies apprehend their strengths and weaknesses

The range of people suffering from the illness has extended dramatically in recent years, and the sizable style of times has expanded even more. Learning, behavior, and stylish high-quality of existence may additionally all be considerably impacted with the aid of ADHD, a neurodevelopmental sickness.

Sadly, women with ADHD regularly revel in fantastic boundaries in evaluation to their male opposite numbers, collectively with acquiring an ADHD assessment later in lifestyles, fewer remedy options, and more horrific stigma. In order to beautify the high-quality of existence for women with ADHD, it's far critical to pay interest on assisting them in records their strengths and shortcomings.

Assessing a lady's requirements is the first step in assisting her recognize her strengths and shortcomings if she has ADHD. A thorough evaluation with a psychologist or precise highbrow health professional may be used to accomplish this. An examination of the children's social competencies, giant well-being, and educational achievement have to all be part of this approach. The exam must additionally deal with recognizing the kid's belongings and liabilities, which incorporates regions of energy or regions of issue. This evaluation serves due to the fact the cornerstone for comprehending each female's precise necessities and may guide the introduction of a suitable remedy approach.

When the evaluation is over, interest have to take delivery of to supporting girls with ADHD in information their strengths and shortcomings. Many strategies, collectively with character or group remedy, social capabilities improvement, and educational treatments, may be used to attain this.

It's critical to focus on the kid's features, along side resilience and inventiveness, while furthermore supporting her in identifying and coping with her flaws. For example, a counsellor can also help the teen in identifying her impulsivity and terrible time management competencies, after which help her provide you with control solutions. Also, on the way to growth the kid's resilience and self guarantee, it is crucial to pay interest on assisting them include and rate themselves.

In order to assist girls with ADHD achieve their complete capability, it's also essential to provide them the proper motels and resource. Extended check time, specialized training, and get admission to to assistive technology are a few examples of lodges. Giving emotional manual and direction is especially critical considering ladies with ADHD regularly battle with precise emotional issues together with tension, depression, and terrible self-esteem. This may be completed through family treatment, discern education, individual counselling, and group counselling.

Lastly, it is critical to provide assist and tools to dad and mom and exceptional caregivers of women who've ADHD. Learning about ADHD, its effects on girls, and the manner to offer appropriate adjustments and allows can be beneficial for parents. In order to engage with different mother and father who're in similar situations, parents may additionally furthermore benefit from using aid networks like on-line boards and help businesses. These tool can also moreover offer dad and mom a feel of camaraderie, educate them, and lead them to sense much less by myself.

Improving the best of lifestyles for ladies with ADHD consists of helping them in spotting their strengths and shortcomings. It is essential to become privy to every children's unique necessities, positioned an emphasis on supporting the kid in knowledge his or her strengths and limitations, provide the proper lodges and allows, and allow parents and caregivers get entry to to equipment and assist.

Girls with ADHD may additionally moreover growth the competencies and self-assurance they need to stay a fulfillment and pleasing lives through way of the use of following the ones suggestions.

Teaching coping strategies for hard conditions

For many mother and father, it is probably hard to elevate a daughter who has Attention Deficit Hyperactivity Disorder (ADHD). Focus, impulse manipulate, and emotion management issues introduced on by way of way of using ADHD also can moreover make it tough to address hard instances.

Because of this, parents of women with ADHD can experience overburdened and dubious of a manner to help their daughter. Parents who observe coping techniques for hard occasions also can furthermore better help their daughters in the course of these attempting instances.

The reputation quo of a regular and straightforward environment is step one in education coping mechanisms. This consists of establishing limits, allowing children to explicit their emotions, and giving shape and balance. Daughters can be capable of make plans and apprehend what to anticipate while dad and mom are regular and structured. The burden of getting to typically adapt to severa expectations may be lessened via way of doing this. Moreover, allowing youngsters to express their feelings and installation limits may additionally moreover make them enjoy heard and valued and beautify their capability to address hard instances.

When a solid and sincere placing has been created, it's miles essential to impart coping mechanisms. Children who're capable of cope with hard activities may additionally better control their emotions and sentiments. Examples of coping techniques embody deep respiration, counting to 10, taking a harm from the scenario, and having a "time-out". Parents can also additionally help their daughter come to be extra emotionally aware and further prepared to control difficult occasions via education coping mechanisms.

In addition to coaching coping abilties, it's far important to educate problem-solving abilities. Children who are unique at hassle-solving may also find out the foundation in their problems and provide you with solutions. Parents may additionally furthermore help their daughter in locating the problem's root cause, growing with remedies, and weighing the benefits and disadvantages of each approach. Children that do this can be higher capable of find out the premise in their troubles and devise answers.

Ultimately, it's miles important to teach emotional control competencies. Children who've the potential to find out and manipulate their feelings are said to have emotional manipulate capabilities. This may be completed by manner of coaching college students in mindfulness practices, inclusive of taking a minute to look at their respiration or naming and labelling their feelings. Parents may additionally additionally encourage their daughter to find out new techniques for coping with their feelings, which consist of talking to themselves absolutely or finding distractions.

Parents who train their daughters coping techniques might also moreover assist them offer their daughter the guide she needs to get via those trying instances. Parents can also moreover help their daughter in better managing her feelings and obtaining the competencies had to deal with tough activities thru manner of fostering a climate of safety and agree with and education coping mechanisms, trouble-solving techniques, and emotional regulation abilties. Girls with ADHD might also additionally expand the competencies needed to efficiently address hard instances and feature glad, wholesome lives with the proper help.

Chapter 3: Developing Social Skills

Helping women make buddies and construct relationships

It is probably difficult to guide a girl with Attention Deficit Hyperactivity Disorder (ADHD) in forming friendships and growing connections, however it is vital to keep this in mind. Making a distinction to your daughter's life is feasible with the perfect strategies.

Creating an surroundings that encourages open communication and listening is one of the maximum vital subjects you can do to help your daughter with ADHD in making buddies and growing connections. You may additionally accomplish this thru making sure that your daughter's voice is heard and valued, no matter how little or trivial her perspectives or critiques may also moreover additionally seem. Encourage her to speak about her emotions and passions whilst being cautious to take note of her with out passing judgement.

Also, it is critical to actively inspire your daughter to interact in pastimes that she likes and at the manner to beneficial useful resource in her forming friendships. If she desires to play sports activities or be part of a membership or agency, as an example, sign her up and deliver her the aid and motivation she wants to prevail. She will gain social talents and be able to set up connections as a give up stop result.

Giving your daughter with ADHD normal form and course is every different crucial step in assisting her broaden friendships and connections. She may be higher capable of control herself and apprehend what is required of her because of this. Having a normal everyday and expectations may also even assist her to stay prepared and targeted.

Also, it is essential to praise your daughter for top notch conduct and supply her praise. She becomes happy with herself and recognize that she is able to exceeding expectations because of this.

Lastly, it's crucial to make certain your infant has opportunities to engage along side her classmates. Make an try to agenda playdates or other sports activities with children her age, and ensure that they're below individual supervision. This will make certain that she is in a regular placing and connecting with classmates who should turn out to be her buddies.

Making buddies and putting in connections collectively with your daughter who has ADHD is probably difficult, however it's miles potential with the right strategies. In order to encourage her to engage in subjects she likes, offer her with regular form and supervision, provide high-quality reinforcement and prizes, and deliver her opportunity to have interaction collectively with her classmates, make certain you set up an environment that encourages open conversation and listening. With these property, you may considerably effect your daughter's lifestyles.

Teaching conversation skills

Girls with ADHD can also have trouble controlling their emotions, forming and retaining relationships, and successfully speakme with others. For more younger women to acquire lifestyles and recognize their complete capability, verbal exchange competencies education is essential.

Prior to whatever else, it's miles important to recognize the underlying cause for any communique troubles those girls may be having. Due to its impulsivity and hassle concentrating, ADHD may additionally impede the improvement of communication abilities.

Girls with ADHD are extra vulnerable to being sidetracked, which makes it difficult for them to attention on art work or pay interest all through discussions. They can also be impulsive, which reasons them to speak without questioning or lose manipulate of their feelings. Girls with ADHD can also lack social competencies, making it tough for them to conform with discussions or choose up on social signs and symptoms and signs and symptoms.

The next stage is to create strategies to assist the girls in obtaining the suitable communication competencies as quickly due to the fact the underlying purpose of the verbal exchange problems has been recognized. It's essential to offer a welcoming surroundings in which the ladies can also moreover training their conversation talents. For example, make certain that the talks are not too drawn-out or difficult to have a look at.

Also, it is critical to permit the ladies a while to think in advance than replying and to provide encouragement once they make strides.

Giving girls with ADHD the opportunity to schooling their conversation competencies is a crucial aspect of training them. Role-gambling video games are one viable way to educate the women the manner to attend to interactions with others and rehearse severa situations. It's essential to offer the ladies the possibility to eavesdrop on discussions and ask questions about various communication techniques. They can also have a better draw near of appropriate communique as a stop result.

It's vital to pay attention on imparting ladies with ADHD with the tools they need to control their emotions. Among various things, this includes coaching youngsters within the recognition and right expression of their emotions. Also, giving the ladies tools to assist them stay centered, which encompass using seen aids or breaking subjects down into smaller pieces, may additionally moreover assist them stay on the proper song and be extra powerful.

Lastly, at the same time as coaching communication abilities to ladies with ADHD, it's far critical to be expertise and affected man or woman. Girls with ADHD can also moreover have trouble grasping ideas and soaking up data, and it may take them some time to accumulate and increase the essential talents. Also, it is vital to offer encouragement and widely recognized the women' accomplishments and growth.

To assist women with ADHD apprehend their whole functionality and attain lifestyles, it's miles essential to educate them verbal exchange talents. These girls might also gain the required conversation skills to manual their success with the useful aid of comprehending the underlying reasons of the troubles, growing a pleasing surroundings for the women to schooling their abilties, and being affected character and empathetic with the ladies.

Addressing Problems with Bullying and Rejection

A severe problem that has currently grown more and more commonplace is the bullying and rejection of girls with ADHD. In a survey performed in 2020, 17% of women with ADHD recommended having been the goal of bullying or rejection from their peers. This truth ought to be taken carefully even as you preserve in mind that rejection and bullying can also have destructive effects on every the victims and their friends. In sure times, it can bring about depression, low vanity, social isolation, and suicidal thoughts.

Bullying and rejection of girls with ADHD are issues which can be normally disregarded or unnoticed considering that they will be usually belief of as usual components of growing up. Yet on account that rejection and bullying also can additionally have very volatile outcomes, taking movement to deal with the problem is critical. Also, faculties must attempt to promote a way of life in which absolutely everyone is dealt with with apprehend and decency.

By supplying expertise and resource to those affected, the problem of bullying and rejection of women with ADHD can also be resolved. Counselling offerings and parental help resources want to be made to be had in colleges for university college college students who've experienced bullying and rejection. In addition to speakme to their kids about bullying, dad and mom can also furthermore assist via way of growing a regular and supportive surroundings at home.

Finally, it's far critical to create an surroundings wherein people with ADHD are understood and handled with compassion. It is feasible to do that thru instructing people approximately ADHD and its results. For youngsters with ADHD, colleges may additionally offer modifications for trying out or provide them greater time to complete their assignments.

By developing a supportive atmosphere, we may additionally additionally help to reduce the stigma and discrimination that human beings with ADHD regularly face.

While it's far a important duty, fighting the problem of female ADHD sufferers being bullied and rejected is hard. By taking steps to create a steady and inclusive ecosystem, providing property and help, and developing an thoughts-set of empathy and statistics, we're able to limit the threat of bullying and rejection of ADHD girls and make certain they may be dealt with with apprehend and dignity.

Chapter 4: Managing Symptoms And Behavior

Understanding ADHD Medications

Sadly, for the cause that symptoms of ADHD in girls might in all likelihood variety from those in boys, it's miles regularly not properly recognized. Daydreaming, inattention, and forgetfulness are common signs of ADHD in ladies, who regularly have a greater slight version of the illness. Moreover, ladies also can conflict with social connections, time control, and business enterprise.

Understanding the diverse remedies which can be available is critical because of the particular troubles which can be related to ADHD in ladies. One of the maximum well-known sorts of remedy for ADHD in every women and boys is medicine. While choosing a medicinal drug for an ADHD woman, there are various factors that have to be taken into thoughts.

Stimulants and non-stimulants are the 2 sorts of pills which is probably most customarily used to deal with ADHD in ladies. The most popular ADHD tablets are stimulants, which act through raising dopamine and norepinephrine levels in the thoughts. These drugs might also moreover lessen impulsivity and increase interest in ADHD kids. The stimulants Ritalin, Adderall, Vayarin, and Concerta are common.

Another shape of drug used to cope with ADHD in ladies is non-stimulants. These drugs feature via elevating the concentrations of various brain chemical substances like serotonin and norepinephrine. To offer a greater properly-rounded path of remedy, non-stimulants are frequently blended with stimulants. Typical non-stimulants are Kapvay, Intuniv, and Strattera.

Psychotherapy, behaviour remedy, and way of lifestyles changes are feasible additional remedy plans for ADHD in ladies outdoor capsules. Psychotherapy can also help women with ADHD apprehend and manage their signs and signs and symptoms and symptoms, and behavior remedy can assist them discover ways to higher modify their emotions and movements. Do greater exercise, eat a wholesome weight loss plan, and get adequate sleep are some examples of way of lifestyles enhancements.

It's crucial to don't forget a female's particular requirements and alternatives on the identical time as deciding on a remedy for her ADHD. Also, it is essential to go through any dangers and side effects with her scientific health practitioner. Drugs can be useful in treating ADHD in ladies, but for the awesome effects, they must be used with wonderful treatment and manner of lifestyles modifications.

Girls with ADHD may be tough to turn out to be privy to and deal with, however with the best care, they could learn how to manipulate their signs and function happy, successful lives. Parents may additionally moreover make sure their daughter has the greatest care with the aid of being aware of the severa remedy alternatives which is probably to be had.

Overview of drugs Options

The most famous treatment for ADHD is remedy, and there are various extremely good forms of capsules available on the market. An assessment of the diverse drug alternatives for girls with ADHD may be given in this text.

Stimulants

The most usually given drugs for ADHD are stimulants. Stimulants feature by using way of boosting ranges of the neurotransmitters dopamine and norepinephrine within the mind, which allows to boom interest and decrease hyperactivity. They had been showed to be useful in decreasing symptoms and signs and symptoms and signs and signs and symptoms in each boys and women with ADHD, and they may be regularly properly-tolerated. Methylphenidate (Ritalin, Concerta, and Daytrana) and amphetamines are traditional stimulants (Adderall and Vyvanse).

Non-stimulants

Non-stimulant pills are regularly used to deal with ADHD in female sufferers. These drugs function differently from stimulants and interest on high-quality neurotransmitters inside the mind. Clonidine, guanfacine (Intuniv), and atomoxetine (Strattera) are examples of commonplace non-stimulants (Kapvay). Girls with ADHD who do now not react to or have hassle tolerating stimulants are frequently administered non-stimulants.

Antidepressants

Antidepressants are on occasion used to address ADHD in women, specifically the ones who have comorbid anxiety or depression. The antidepressants bupropion (Wellbutrin) and fluoxetine are frequently used to address ADHD (Prozac). Despite the truth that the ones tablets are regularly well ordinary and capable of lowering symptoms and signs and symptoms, they may moreover motive a few very risky unfavourable results.

herbal remedies

Girls with ADHD are increasingly more turning to herbal remedies as a remedy. Due to the paucity of facts proving their efficacy, herbal treatment alternatives aren't FDA-regular and aren't advised as first-line treatments. Ginkgo biloba, chamomile, and lavender are not unusual herbs used to cope with ADHD.

changes in healthy dietweight-reduction plan and way of life

In addition to treatment, food and manner of existence adjustments can also additionally help women with ADHD sense higher. Symptoms may be lessened by using the use of consuming a balanced diet regime, maintaining off processed materials and chocolates, and getting sufficient of rest. Exercise is also useful for the purpose that it can useful useful resource with hyperactivity and hobby. In addition, it's miles vital to make sure that girls with ADHD get a number of social assist and tremendous complaint.

There are many specific types of tablets that can be used to deal with ADHD, it definitely is a everyday and curable infection. The most often encouraged capsules for ADHD are stimulants, however there are also non-stimulants, antidepressants, and natural remedies. Dietary and manner of lifestyles adjustments can also be useful in decreasing symptoms and signs in addition to medicinal drug. Finding the superior route of movement for every precise girl calls for discussing all to be had remedies with a scientific expert.

Tips for treatment control

ADHD is often dealt with with treatment, however it's far important to apprehend the manner to address it in ladies. Here are some suggestions for treatment control in women with ADHD.

1. Create a recurring: Making an attempt to hold a everyday agenda will assist to ensure that medication is taken as directed. This is vital for ladies with ADHD particularly due to the fact they will be much more likely to overlook to take their medicine. Girls taking the proper dose on the proper time can also be helped with the aid of using a ordinary.

2. Keep a watch fixed out for issue effects: Because remedy might also additionally have them, it's far vital to hold an eye fixed out for any changes in mood or behaviour. It's essential to maintain a watch out for any signs of viable issues due to the fact ladies with ADHD may be

extra at risk of pharmaceutical component effects.

3. Consult your clinical medical doctor: It's crucial to searching for advice out of your physician if you have any queries or problems regarding your daughter's medicinal drug. On the manner to because it ought to be manipulate medicinal drug in women with ADHD, they'll offer hints and path.

4. Take dietary adjustments underneath consideration: Since excellent food and dietary supplements might also additionally additionally warfare with unique tablets, it is vital to talk on your scientific doctor in advance than making any nutritional changes. For example, it is not in truth beneficial to mix grapefruit juice with numerous ADHD tablets.

5. Track development: When your daughter is receiving medication, it is important to track her development. This involves maintaining a be careful for changes in her behaviour, attitude, or educational success. It's moreover vital to show any negative outcomes she is probably having.

6. Invest in help: To help your daughter manage her ADHD, it's far vital to spend money on supporting services like treatment or counselling. This may additionally additionally furthermore help to assure that she is receiving the finest care possible and might help to lower the opportunity of any viable pharmaceutical awful results.

7. Educate yourself: It's vital to teach your self on ADHD if you're going to address a lady's remedy. This entails being informed about the various commands of drugs, their destructive effects, and the manner to manipulate them effectively.

You can assure that your daughter is receiving the brilliant feasible deal with her ADHD by means of manner of the use of being attentive to the recommendation in this article. It's essential to keep in thoughts that controlling ADHD in ladies also can want unique strategies further to remedy, which incorporates counselling and remedy.

You can also furthermore help your daughter in leading a extra a success and meaningful existence by manner of taking the time to govern her drug treatments accurately.

Chapter 5: Implementing Behavioral Strategies

Positive reinforcement strategies

Girls with ADHD frequently enjoy troubles in faculty, domestic, and social settings. As a end result, it's miles vital for mother and father and caregivers to apply first-rate reinforcement techniques to assist these women manage their ADHD signs and symptoms and signs.

Positive reinforcement techniques are strategies used to reward great behaviour. Positive reinforcement helps ladies with ADHD construct properly coping competencies and encourages great behaviour. It moreover lets in to lessen difficult behaviours and increases vanity.

One way to use powerful reinforcement is thru verbal reward. Verbal reward is an powerful way to reward proper behaviour. Every time a girl with ADHD demonstrates a favored behaviour, it is vital to praise her for it. You ought to mention a few thing like, "I'm so happy with you for finishing your homework on time," if she completes her assignments on time. This will encourage her to comprehend that her behavior is actual and desired.

Another a hit high excellent reinforcement technique is providing prizes. Rewards may be used to beautify preferred behaviours. For example, if a woman with ADHD cleans her room without being requested, you can thank her with a special deal with or a completely unique tour. This will help her to understand that her efforts are valued.

It's crucial to offer ladies with ADHD shape and consistency further to verbal reward and rewards. This will help women with ADHD to recognize what to expect and will help them discover ways to control their ADHD signs and symptoms and signs and signs and symptoms.

Finally, wonderful reinforcement techniques must be utilized in combination with different techniques. For instance, it's miles crucial to also incorporate behavioural treatment. Girls with ADHD will benefit from this sort of treatment considering that it will teach them a manner to come to be aware about their triggers and manipulate their signs and symptoms and symptoms. In addition, it is important to make certain that girls with ADHD get enough sleep and physical activity. These factors will help to lessen pressure and growth interest.

Generally, high-quality reinforcement techniques are an first rate technique to assist women with ADHD manipulate their signs. These tactics are critical for enhancing proper actions, improving conceitedness, and supporting females with ADHD perceive their triggers.

It is vital to use remarkable reinforcement strategies in tandem with other treatments collectively with behavioural treatment, suitable sleep, and physical workout. All of these strategies will help women with ADHD lead greater wholesome and additional green lives.

Punishment Alternatives

From the instances of spankings and time-outs, one of a kind kinds of punishment for ADHD girls have superior notably. In the current-day-

day worldwide, parents are more involved with using optimistic complaint to help their daughters adjust their behaviour. Although traditional sanctions are in spite of the reality that an opportunity, dad and mom have to look for greater effective substitutes if you want to educate their girls to make higher choices and higher manipulate their ADHD symptoms.

Offering prizes for suitable behavior is one of the top notch punishment alternatives for ADHD girls. Rewards can consist of things like a special deal with, more time to do some trouble they enjoy, or a completely unique privilege.

This can be a splendid manner to encourage them to make clever selections and renowned their achievements. The rewards want to be suitable for their daughter's age and diploma of functionality, and they should now not be excessively big.

Another powerful punishment possibility for ADHD ladies is to offer them with fantastic reinforcement. When they do nicely, you may do this through complimenting them verbally or thru the use of offering them actual prizes like stickers or little toys. This can help to assemble self-esteem and inspire high amazing behaviour.

Parents also can offer creative punishments for ADHD ladies. One of those may be making them write an apology letter or lead them to complete a mission they loathe. The concept is to offer them an opportunity to take a look at a lesson with out using physical pressure.

Parents can also lease natural effects to deal with misbehaviour in ADHD girls. For instance, if a daughter does no longer do her chores, then she can also additionally must bypass with out some element she enjoys till the chore is finished. This can help to train her that there are consequences to her movements and that she needs to take duty for her options.

Finally, parents also can use trouble-fixing techniques whilst handling their ADHD daughters. This consists of encouraging their daughter to count on thru the hassle and give you an answer. They can help their daughter take a look at better preference-making abilities and the manner to weigh the professionals and cons of her alternatives with the resource of coaching her hassle-solving techniques.

Ultimately, there are quite diverse diverse punishment opportunities for ADHD ladies that might assist to address their behaviour in an super way. Parents have to search for strategies to encourage their daughter to make better selections and to understand their accomplishments.

To help their daughter higher manage her ADHD signs and signs and symptoms and signs and symptoms and learn how to make better selections, they may make use of rewards, remarkable reinforcement, innovative punishments, herbal results, and problem-fixing strategies.

Using mindfulness and rest techniques

It is generally acknowledged that humans with interest deficit hyperactivity illness could possibly advantage from schooling mindfulness and relaxation practices (ADHD). A series of practices called mindfulness can assist human beings awareness better, deal with strain higher, and experience higher mentally all round. Physical tension and highbrow pressure can every be reduced with relaxation strategies. Both of these techniques may also moreover permit ladies with ADHD to manipulate their signs and symptoms and symptoms and function more green and notable lives.

Mindfulness consists of being gift within the 2nd, with out judgement. It is a way of being attentive to one's thoughts, feelings, and sensations in a non-judgmental way. It may assist women with ADHD to higher manipulate their feelings and control their impulses. Mindfulness also can permit girls with ADHD to be more aware of their feelings and feelings, supporting them to better cope with hard instances.

Girls with ADHD can schooling mindfulness through meditation, yoga, and distinct rest techniques. Meditation may additionally additionally assist to decrease strain, improve hobby, and enhance mood. It includes sitting quietly and concentrating on the breath or an item. With meditation, ladies with ADHD can also learn how to study their thoughts without responding to them. Yoga is a few other awesome approach to domesticate mindfulness. It can assist to reduce stress and anxiety, beautify hobby, and boom interest of the frame and thoughts.

Relaxation techniques also are effective for women with ADHD. Relaxation strategies which consist of slow muscle relaxation, deep breathing, and guided visualisation can also help to relieve bodily and intellectual stress. Progressive muscle rest includes tensing after which releasing each muscle organization in order. This can also furthermore help to relieve tension and increase hobby. Deep respiration and guided imagery contain focusing at the breath and visualising calming pics and scenes. These strategies can beneficial aid in focusing better and reducing pressure.

In addition to mindfulness and relaxation practices, ladies with ADHD may additionally advantage from way of life changes. Eating a healthy weight loss program, getting ordinary exercising, and getting enough sleep can all help to enhance attention and reduce stress. Establishing wholesome sleep behavior and keeping off espresso may moreover help to boom interest and restrict impulsivity.

Lastly, women with ADHD may probably gain from speaking to a therapist. A therapist can help ladies to pick out and manipulate their signs and symptoms and signs and symptoms, further to offer aid and steering. A therapist also can allow girls to bring together coping strategies that may allow them to higher manage their signs.

Mindfulness and rest techniques can be powerful for ladies with ADHD. These strategies can resource in stress reduction and recognition development. Girls with ADHD may additionally additionally manage their symptoms and enjoy extra a achievement and enormous lives thru making way of existence adjustments and speaking to a therapist.

Chapter 6: Addressing School Challenges

Communicating with instructors and school Administrators

For mother and father of women with ADHD, speaking with teachers and directors can be hard. There are wonderful massive suggestions and procedures that parents may use to efficaciously advocate for their daughter's instructional needs, despite the fact that each teenager is precise and could have exquisite desires.

First, it's miles vital for dad and mom to initiate conversations with instructors and university officers. Before any troubles emerge, communicate to the trainer or the pinnacle of the university. Tell the college approximately your daughter's contamination and inquire approximately what the faculty can do to assist. In order for their daughter to be triumphant inside the university, mother and father need to moreover communicate approximately any precise lodges or adjustments that would be required. In the destiny, this can assist offer the concept for powerful verbal exchange.

Second, it is crucial for mother and father to reveal their daughter's academic fulfillment. A not unusual file on her normal normal overall performance in elegance and on assessments want to be requested from the trainer or school management. These updates will permit parents to look any capability hassle regions and to take early motion.

Finally, it's miles crucial for dad and mom to keep composure and courtesy while talking with teachers and university officers. While navigating the sorts of public colleges is probably ugly, elevating your voice or being aggressive will no longer help the scenario. It is also important to word that teachers and faculty officers are regularly walking with restricted resources and might not be able to supply the degree of assist that dad and mom may also want to determine on.

Fourth, dad and mom can also discover it beneficial to collaborate with the school to create a method for assisting their daughter. This motion plan has to encompass particular modifications in an effort to manual her success further to study room behaviour techniques. Inquire about the opinions of the faculty's management, teachers, and one of a type parents who've handled ADHD.

Lastly, make certain to incorporate your daughter within the dialogue. Ask her how she feels within the study room and what techniques had been a fulfillment for her. Urge her to take part in the communique and permit her recognize how vital her opinion is.

For dad and mom of women with ADHD, speaking with teachers and administrators may be tough. However, dad and mom can correctly suggest for his or her daughter's academic wishes by manner of being proactive, final knowledgeable, final calm and respectful, running together to expand a plan, and regarding their daughter within the verbal exchange.

Supporting educational achievement

The intellectual disorder called ADHD, which can also have an impact on each adults and youngsters, may moreover have a tremendous terrible have an impact on on someone's academic achievement. While ADHD is extra huge in grownup adult adult males than in women, it may although considerably have an effect on girls' educational ordinary standard overall performance.

It can be difficult for girls with ADHD to stay up academically because of the truth they often have problems with employer, cognizance, and impulsivity. Thankfully, there are a number of actions that parents, educators, and distinct adults can take to support the instructional success of girls with ADHD.

Providing the right gadget and assistance is one of the maximum critical subjects parents can do to help girls with ADHD acquire achievement academically. This might also encompass giving the lady a train or more assist from a instructor or helper. It may additionally entail acquiring get right of get admission to to to instructional assets or generation that could assist her better manage her ADHD signs. A female with ADHD, for example, would benefit from the usage of an app that maintains her focused or an electronic organiser to stay organized. Adults want to also ensure the lady has get proper of access to to intellectual health remedies, including remedy or remedy, if important.

The female goals a supportive environment from adults if you need to acquire her instructional desires. This also can encompass encouraging her and boosting her arrogance. Additionally, it is vital to offer her with techniques and set inexpensive expectancies. For instance, adults might also help the girl lessen onerous chores into smaller, less complex-to-control segments. Adults also can encourage the child through giving her praise while she accomplishes her goals.

It's crucial to verify that the woman is aware about her jail rights regarding schooling. In the observe room and on examinations, women with ADHD can be certified for positive lodges and modifications. They can also be entitled for added time for examinations and assignments. Adults need to make sure that the lady's instructors are aware of her rights and assist her in statistics them.

Lastly, adults want to aid the woman in growing effective examine behavior. This might probably encompass assisting her with organizing her belongings and training her how to put together in advance for responsibilities and checks. The toddler must be encouraged through adults to divide her art work into smaller quantities and to establish clean goals for each pastime. Adults should moreover assist the child in installing region a distraction-free have a have a take a look at area and make sure that she takes not unusual breaks.

Girls with ADHD are capable of attaining their instructional goals and realising their whole functionality with the precise assist and path.

Addressing homework and organisational problems

It can be specifically tough for kids to control their schoolwork thinking about that they often locate it difficult to live organized and be privy to chores. Their instructional overall performance and well-known well-being may additionally additionally moreover undergo as a give up quit end result.

Homework and organisational troubles might be mainly tough for an ADHD woman. Many girls with ADHD conflict with time control and attention, which may be mainly hard in terms of doing their schoolwork. They also can battle to maintain based and have a look at thru on their commitments. In addition, many girls with ADHD lack the strength of mind required to complete assignments and keep instructional progress.

Parents and educators also can provide manual and route so you can help with those disturbing situations. It's crucial to be supportive and empathetic on the equal time as nevertheless outlining limits and expectancies. Moreover, parents and instructors must model robust organizing skills and provide assist at the same time as required.

Providing shape and regularity is a outstanding approach to help an ADHD toddler cope with her schoolwork and organisational stressful conditions. It is probably useful to create a everyday homework recurring and designate a selected time and place for homework. Also, it is essential that parents and instructors be reachable to the female that lets in you to offer help, route, and to maintain her on path.

It additionally may be beneficial to divide sports into smaller, less difficult-to-control quantities. For instance, breaking down a top mission into smaller portions may help the female feel more on pinnacle of factors and less beaten.

It may also be useful to provide visible clues to help the lady maintain in thoughts her responsibilities. She may also furthermore maintain her business enterprise and consciousness via making use of a tick list or calendar, for example. Additionally, giving her reminders finally of the day can useful resource in maintaining her centered.

It's critical to encourage the girl to take breaks and participate in matters she likes in addition to providing form and assist. She can keep focused and recommended thru taking common breaks from her assignments. She can also take a damage and preserve her motivation by way of the usage of way of taking part in matters she likes, like playing sports activities sports sports or exploring her creativity.

Last but no longer least, it is crucial to have staying power and knowledge. It is probably hard for an ADHD girl to preserve prepared and centered, so it is crucial to offer assistance and be sympathetic to any demanding situations she may probable have.

Although coping with an ADHD female's organisational and schoolwork troubles is probably difficult, it's miles feasible with the proper help and course. Parents and instructors may useful resource an ADHD girl's potential to stay centered and stimulated by means of way of manner of putting in place shape and ordinary, dividing work into viable quantities, the usage of seen cues, and taking commonplace pauses. Also, for you to provide the best help viable, it's far important to live upbeat and sympathetic.

Chapter 7: Navigating Life Transitions

Preparing for Puberty and Adolescence

All teenagers experience numerous physical and emotional adjustments all through teenagers. It is probably specifically hard for girls with Attention Deficit Hyperactivity Disorder (ADHD) to adjust to puberty and childhood. Girls with ADHD frequently battle to manipulate their emotions and conduct, which offers massive stress to the state of affairs.

Thankfully, there are strategies to resource in their training. With a bit steering and knowledge, mother and father and caregivers can provide the help that women with ADHD need inside the course of this hard length.

Understanding what an ADHD woman is experiencing is step one in helping her in getting geared up for puberty and youth. Girls are stricken by ADHD in a awesome manner than grownup men are, and their signs and symptoms may additionally once in a while be more severe. Impulsivity and hassle handling rage are extra not unusual in ladies with ADHD. They can also warfare with horrible shallowness and enjoy overburdened thru their academic and social obligations. The first step in assisting ladies with ADHD in getting geared up for the adjustments that occur with puberty is understanding the particular problems with ADHD and the way it influences them.

Once the dad and mom of an ADHD lady understand the problems she is experiencing, the following step is to assist her put together for the physical adjustments that get up with puberty. This includes talking approximately deodorant and menstruation merchandise, in addition to the fundamentals of cleanliness. Make positive she is familiar with the way to use these things efficiently and has get entry to to them at the same time as required.

Parents must additionally speak with their daughter the physical adjustments related to puberty, together with the boom of breast tissue, frame hair, and frame odour. The woman may moreover experience higher prepared and lots less crushed after speaking approximately those modifications.

Girls with ADHD want to be ready for the emotional and social modifications that stand up with early life similarly to the physical ones. For women with ADHD who may additionally war with self-law and social engagement, the ones transitions can be in particular tough.

She can higher technique her mind and emotions and get the coping mechanisms she goals if you speak to the woman about them. She can manage her emotions more healthily if you assist her adopt self-care practices like journaling, exercising, and relaxation strategies.

Girls with ADHD should have a supportive circle of relatives environment, consistent with their dad and mom. This could possibly encompass giving her a smooth framework and ordinary in addition to permitting her room to express herself. Encourage her to participate in pastimes she exhibits fun, together with track, portray, or athletics. She might also specific her emotions and experience a enjoy of achievement thru taking element in the ones sports, which can also function a release for her.

Lastly, dad and mom of girls with ADHD want to be aware about the risks related to puberty. It's important to be privy to those dangers and overtly talk them with the child because of the truth that women with ADHD are extra prone to take part in unstable behaviours like drug use and early sexual involvement. In addition, parents should be privy to the signs and signs of disappointment and anxiety and are looking for for help while crucial.

Adolescence can be a demanding length for all kids, however it is able to be specifically trying for girls with ADHD. With a chunk training and reputation, dad and mom can provide the assist and advice that women with ADHD need to navigate this tough duration. Parents can also additionally assist their daughter in getting ready for the problems of youth via the use of speaking to them about the physical, emotional, and social changes that arise with puberty, developing a secure home environment, and being privy to feasible threats.

Talking about body changes and intercourse training

The trouble of sex schooling for girls with ADHD is crucial and shouldn't be neglected. Parents and instructors need to apprehend the ideal requirements of ladies with ADHD and offer them the right data approximately their our our bodies and sexual health.

Girls with Attention Deficit Hyperactivity Disorder (ADHD) can discover it more difficult than their classmates to recognise, alter, and particular their feelings. Girls with ADHD can also additionally struggle to pay attention and maintain statistics, which may also negatively impact their social and academic trendy normal performance.

In addition, unstable behaviours inclusive of early sexual involvement and drug addiction may be more not unusual in ladies with ADHD.

Girls with ADHD may additionally need more help although the identical troubles as the ones for people with out ADHD may be furnished in sex education applications. This is because of the possibility that they may not recognize the material further to their classmates do, and the possibility that they'll be more likely to act riskily.

It's crucial to offer ladies with ADHD accurate, age suitable information even as talking approximately intercourse. Also, it's essential to exercising persistence and compassion due to the reality women with ADHD may additionally need extra time to take in and recognise new information. Also, it is important to talk to ladies about the possible effects of early sexual engagement and provide them contraceptive options.

It's crucial to talk approximately the potential physical adjustments that girls may work thru throughout puberty further to beginning manage. All teenage ladies might also moreover enjoy confusion for the duration of puberty, however people with ADHD may moreover want greater help and counselling. It is critical to talk approximately the potential bodily, highbrow, and social adjustments associated with puberty and to strain the need for self-care.

It's additionally vital to have nonjudgmental and independent conversations about sex and sexuality. It's crucial to provide a stable and inspiring surroundings for ladies with ADHD for you to unique their mind and ask questions on their sexuality. Girls with ADHD can also have worries approximately their personal sexuality. It's important to pressure that sex and intimacy are important factors of life and want to be skilled in a healthful, consenting way.

Last but not least, it's miles important to emphasise to women with ADHD that they may be able to making realistic judgments and that they have the freedom to determine on the same time as and the manner to take part in sexual hobby. It is essential to pressure that women with ADHD have the right to refuse social pressure and one-of-a-kind varieties of coercion for the purpose that they will be more at risk of them. Their choices ought to moreover be respectable.

All subjects taken into consideration, sex training for women with ADHD is a crucial trouble that need to no longer be overlooked. Girls want to get accurate and age-appropriate statistics from dad and mom and instructors, and they want to foster a secure surroundings wherein they revel in at ease speaking approximately their very very own our our bodies and sexual fitness. Girls with ADHD are capable of making realistic and healthful options about their sexuality with the appropriate help and route.

Preparing for emotional and social modifications

Girls' social and emotional development may be substantially impacted with the useful resource of using ADHD, so it's far essential for parents to recognize the symptoms and work with the lady to assist her be prepared for the changes which might be coming.

Discussing the analysis with a female is the first step in helping her in getting prepared for the emotional and social modifications introduced on via the use of ADHD. It's crucial to permit her understand she's not by myself and to talk to her about any remedy alternatives and coping mechanisms that might be to be had. Girls want to be aware that they may be in a function to talk to someone if they're feeling careworn out or beaten.

It's additionally critical to emphasise that, notwithstanding wonderful issues, ADHD will also be a energy since it fosters creativity, mind, and resilience.

Parents want to address helping the kid in developing strategies for controlling her emotions as quickly as the analysis has been disclosed. This can also embody developing relaxation talents, exercising mindfulness, and spotting the motives of emotional outbursts. Girls have to discover ways to discover their emotions and specific them in a healthy way, including through using writing in a pocket e book or speakme with a dependable grownup.

Assisting a woman in developing shallowness is some other essential step in helping her in turning into prepared for the social adjustments added on by means of ADHD. This may be finished with the useful aid of encouraging her to interact in matters that she loves, together with athletics, portray, or tune. Also, parents want to congratulate their children on their accomplishments and help them.

It's crucial to manual her in figuring out her property and provide her the belongings she desires to engage socially collectively along with her classmates.

It's vital to useful resource a female in identifying and pursuing her pursuits further to assisting her increase coping mechanisms for handling her feelings and growing conceitedness. For example, if she loves to take a look at, inspire her to find out new authors and novels. Help her find out possibilities to volunteer and come to be engaged in animal rescue if she loves animals. She also can set up her individuality and learn how to be thrilled together with her unique capabilities and abilties thru pursuing her hobbies.

Lastly, it's far vital to assist a girl with ADHD in getting prepared for the modifications to her social lifestyles. Parents also can speak to their youngsters approximately the fee of making practical selections and growing accurate connections together together with her classmates.

It can be a difficult but pleasurable system to help a woman with ADHD in getting organized for capability emotional and social adjustments in her life. Parents can also moreover help their daughter in establishing coping mechanisms for the outcomes of ADHD and dwelling a a success and first-rate lifestyles thru having a communique approximately the analysis, growing emotional coping mechanisms, boosting arrogance, exploring pursuits, and becoming prepared for social trade.

Managing accelerated duties and independence

Children with ADHD, a disorder referred to as hobby deficit hyperactivity disorder (ADHD), regularly conflict with its signs and symptoms and signs and signs and symptoms and behaviours, leaving many parents and caregivers feeling helpless and overwhelmed. As they will conflict with impulse control, business enterprise, and conversation all of which can be made worse by using the greater independence and duties that encompass maturing ladies with ADHD frequently confront unique troubles.

Thankfully, there are quite a few strategies and strategies that mother and father and specific caregivers may additionally lease to assist women with ADHD in dealing with their growing independence and responsibilities. Keep in thoughts that every girl with ADHD is particular and might need a one in each of a kind strategy.

The maximum essential step is to installation a based definitely place of business. Girls with ADHD might also moreover moreover preserve organization and recognition by way of way of setting barriers and expectancies. Setting a ordinary plan for sports activities activities could likely assist girls with ADHD keep targeted and prepared, helping them to higher deal with their new duties and independence.

Positive reward for top notch behavior is also crucial. A lady's arrogance is boosted on the same time as she receives praise for completing obligations and upholding requirements, which motivates her to keep going for walks hard. Moreover, encouraging ladies with ADHD to keep their desires can be carried out with the aid of the use of way of worthwhile suitable conduct.

Also, it is critical for dad and mom and special adults to be conscious that women with ADHD also can revel in melancholy and feelings of inferiority. It's vital to be sympathetic and galvanizing further to to provide a cushty putting for the lady to express her sentiments.

In order to assist her in dealing with her new responsibilities and independence, it is vital to provide her the proper tool and help from intellectual fitness professionals.

Lastly, it is critical to educate girls with ADHD coping mechanisms for controlling their impulsivity, attention, and energy. It might also assist ladies listen and higher alter their emotions if they're taught mindfulness and relaxation practices. She can continue to be on course and deal with her new duties and independence higher in case you provide her techniques for organizing her art work and breaking them down into smaller, attainable dreams.

It might be tough to address developing independence and obligation in women with ADHD. But, mother and father and caregivers can also help girls with ADHD in succeeding and most important the fine lives possible thru using the ideal system and techniques.

Caregivers may help ladies with ADHD in managing their growing duties and independence in a solid and provoking atmosphere via imparting shape, encouraging feedback, and the essential equipment.

Chapter 8: Transitioning To College And Adulthood

Preparing for the college software method

The university software technique can be an intimidating and difficult revel in for any scholar, however for humans with Attention Deficit Hyperactivity Disorder (ADHD), it is able to be exceedingly scary.

There are some critical strategies that would assist the college utility approach circulate more without problem and correctly for parents of daughters with ADHD who want to get their infant equipped for it.

The most crucial detail is to offer your daughter an organized and inspiring surroundings. This implies which you need to format a particular have a look at schedule that your daughter will comply with every day. Set a time restriction for her to do her schoolwork and examine, and ensure to paste to it. Give her precise, realistic targets that she might also establish for herself and wreck her duties down into small quantities. She is probably capable of preserve targeted and organized thanks to this, that's vital for human beings with ADHD.

It is also crucial to offer your daughter the proper capabilities and resources to acquire fulfillment. This might be some issue from a planner or calendar to a whiteboard for organizing her mind to a computer for filing homework on line. In order to encourage her academically and offer her extra useful aid and path, you can also want to think about hiring a show or mentor. For humans with ADHD, this could be very useful since it enables hold them at the proper song and make certain that they will be mission their goals.

When it includes surely using for university, it is critical to make certain that your daughter is properly-organized. . She need to be informed of her monetary scenario as properly, thinking about the truth that doing so will allow her to make the best selections for her destiny. She should additionally be aware of any scholarships or offers for which she have to qualify, due to the truth the ones may additionally additionally assist defray the price of her schooling and unique fees.

Last but now not least, it's far essential to manual your daughter in studying a manner to manipulate her tension and anxiety all through the college application technique. This is probably taking breaks at some point of the day, workout, or taking part in rest physical video games like deep breathing or meditation. You also can keep in mind asking a representative, the sort of counsellor or therapist, to help you in giving her the help and route she needs.

Overall, the university software machine may be stressful and overwhelming for people with ADHD, but it'd not want to be that way with the proper techniques and useful resource in region. You can assist your daughter in making the most of the college software program program machine and succeeding in her adventure via the usage of giving her a based and inspiring environment, ensuring she has the equipment and assets she wants to gain achievement, and helping her manage her pressure and anxiety inside the course of the approach.

Addressing worrying situations within the college surroundings

For a college pupil with ADHD, the campus placing may additionally offer a whole lot of issues that could avert academic and social fulfillment. With an appropriate help, substances, and inns, the ones problems may be triumph over.

Understanding ADHD and its signs is step one in tackling the issues of a college putting for a scholar with the contamination. ADHD can also make it hard to pay interest, hold organized, manage impulsivity, and manipulate emotions. Understanding how those signs and signs and symptoms may be hurting the scholar's academic everyday performance and social connections is vital that permits you to understand these signs and symptoms.

The subsequent step is to provide a supportive environment for the kid after the signs and symptoms and signs and symptoms and symptoms of ADHD were identified. This includes fostering an environment this is useful to gaining knowledge of further to presenting emotional useful resource and empathy. This can encompass developing a quiet location for gaining knowledge of and lowering interruptions like noise and litter. Developing a method for closing organized, which include utilizing a calendar and setting reminders for duties and tests, can also be beneficial.

By supplying inns and tool, you can assist a pupil with ADHD navigate the problems of a university setting. The pupil can also want greater time to complete obligations or examinations, in addition to assist with taking notes or reading. Make first-class the student has get admission to to any assets that can be to be had, along with tutoring or help for human beings with disabilities. Also, the student need to need changes within the classroom, together with a seat closer the front or authorization to move away the school room in the direction of lectures.

It is likewise essential to set up an surroundings that is inviting and accepting of college students with ADHD. This includes developing a putting in which the scholar feels reliable, favored, and that their goals are being met. Making positive the student's voice is heard, their thoughts are genuine, and their efforts diagnosed may also furthermore all fall below this class. Giving the scholar encouragement for his or her accomplishments, irrespective of how modest, is also useful.

Last but no longer least, it's far important to widely known that treating ADHD can be difficult and to provide the child assist and understanding. This can encompass helping the student in developing coping mechanisms for his or her signs, such techniques for reining in impulsivity and improving attentiveness. Also, it is essential to famend that the student must every now and then need extra assistance or guide and to offer it in a type and sympathetic way.

For a student with ADHD, addressing the issues of a college putting can be a tough manner, but it's far a important one. With the brilliant support, assets, and hotels, it is feasible to installation a welcoming and inclusive environment that lets in the scholar to gain their complete capacity.

Supporting girls in attaining independence and achievement

Boys are much more likely to have ADHD than women, but each sexes may additionally enjoy its devastating results. Girls with ADHD also can have unique difficulties that might restriction their functionality to achieve success and end up impartial.

Girls with ADHD frequently stumble upon numerous challenges on their direction to achievement and independence. First off, youngsters ought to have lousy self-esteem and shortage of self assure because of the stigma that comes with having ADHD.

They can also discover it hard to mention themselves in social settings as a prevent end result, and they may start to distrust their very very personal judgement and capabilities. Girls can also have problem controlling their emotions, which makes it hard to cope with strain and unsightly conditions like war of words.

Also, girls with ADHD may additionally moreover struggle with organization and planning, which can be a prime barrier to independence and fulfillment. Girls who lack organisational talents also can discover it hard to prepare for the destiny, which can also moreover reason them to procrastinate and end up disorganised. Without good enough making plans, women need to discover it tough to prioritise chores and make prolonged-time period plans, which would possibly bring about left out deadlines and misplaced possibilities.

It's crucial to provide a pleasant and data surroundings for girls with ADHD so they'll prevail and emerge as unbiased. Parents, instructors, and exclusive caregivers can also moreover help thru giving shape and supervision to make certain sports are completed on time and by using way of encouraging girls to recognize their strengths and shortcomings. Girls may additionally experience greater prepared and encouraged to achieve their dreams if they'll be endorsed to use wonderful self-speak and to enlarge their self assurance.

Girls must additionally take shipping of the right device and sources to useful beneficial aid in the manage of their signs and signs. For instance, imparting a ordinary every day schedule with reminders can also additionally assist girls maintain prepared and on track.

In addition, giving women organizing gadget like planners, calendars, and to-do lists may additionally useful useful resource in their capability to maintain facts and make plans. Technology also can be used to display development and offer encouragement for completing duties.

Access to appropriate care and remedy for girls is likewise vital. This consists of giving women get admission to to intellectual health treatments like cognitive behavioural therapy so they'll accumulate higher coping mechanisms and control their signs and signs and symptoms. In addition, counselling and medication can be used to govern the signs and symptoms and signs and symptoms of ADHD.

And final, giving girls get proper of get admission to to to a hit role fashions and mentors can be a fantastic technique to guide their fulfillment and independence. Girls who revel in this could gain self-self perception, observe from the mistakes of others, and boom a guide network of others who can relate to and sympathise with their challenges.

In stylish, females with ADHD enjoy some of specific problems that might avert their functionality to turn out to be successful and independent. They can also, however, get thru the ones demanding situations and achieve their dreams with an appropriate assist and materials. Parents, teachers, and one-of-a-type caregivers may additionally moreover assist girls with ADHD in turning into independent and a success through giving them a supportive environment, the proper tool and assets, access to therapy, and correct function fashions.

Chapter 9: Understanding Stubborn Children

Understanding cussed children is essential for parents who're coping with their conduct. It is vital to recognize that a sturdy-willed toddler isn't inherently "terrible" or "difficult," but instead has a very precise persona and way of wondering that calls for a high-quality technique to parenting.

Stubborn youngsters will be inclined to be specifically unbiased and assertive, which could result in electricity struggles with their mother and father. They have a robust enjoy of self and regularly face up to being advised what to do, that may cause them to seem disobedient and defiant.

It is essential to apprehend that stubborn children are not intentionally searching for to be tough, however as an alternative are looking for to assert their independence and control over their environment. They want to be heard and respected, much like every different toddler.

One of the keys to expertise stubborn youngsters is to understand that they have a one-of-a-type mindset on the world than their dad and mom. Parents want to listen to their infant's element of view, no matter the truth that they disagree with it, and validate their emotions. By acknowledging their baby's attitude, mother and father can assemble accept as true with and mutual recognize, that could bring about extra extraordinary interactions.

Another essential detail of knowledge cussed kids is spotting that they have got limits. While they'll seem robust and assured on the outdoor, they although want guidance and help from their dad and mom. Parents must set suitable boundaries and effects for his or her little one's behavior while moreover providing love and guide.

It is also essential for parents to apprehend that stubborn youngsters can be highly sensitive to grievance and can react negatively to perceived criticism. Parents should use terrific reinforcement and praise to inspire their child's amazing conduct, instead of focusing completely on terrible conduct.

Understanding stubborn kids calls for a willingness to see the arena from their mind-set and widely recognized their need for independence and manage. Parents have to offer love and help while additionally placing suitable boundaries and outcomes. By the usage of powerful reinforcement and reward, parents can assist their toddler growth brilliant behaviors and grow to be confident and self-reliant adults.

Why Do Children Become Stubborn?

Stubbornness in kids is a not unusual behavior that is frequently seen throughout their early years of development. While it is a regular trouble of a toddler's increase, excessive stubbornness can motive frustration for both the child and their caregivers. Here are a few functionality reasons of stubbornness in kids:

Developmental stage: Toddlers and preschoolers are simply starting to assert their independence and autonomy. As a result, they'll face up to following instructions and need to do subjects their manner. This can reason stubbornness as they may be searching for to exert manipulate over their surroundings.

Personality traits: Some kids are manifestly more sturdy-willed and decided than others. These tendencies can take area as stubbornness once they enjoy they may be not getting their way.

Fear of change: Children can become connected to exercises and acquainted surroundings. When faced with a contemporary situation or a change in their recurring, they'll turn out to be cussed as a manner of dealing with their worry and uncertainty.

Attention-looking for: Children also can furthermore use cussed behavior as a way of gaining hobby from their caregivers. This is especially real within the event that they experience neglected or not noted.

Lack of verbal exchange abilties: Children won't however have the communication abilties critical to unique their mind and emotions correctly. This can bring about frustration and stubbornness while they may be not able to talk their wishes.

Modeling behavior: Children research through using searching the human beings spherical them. If they see stubborn behavior modeled thru their caregivers or different adults, they will imitate this behavior.

Anxiety or stress: Children who're experiencing tension or strain may additionally moreover furthermore show off cussed behavior as a manner of handling their emotions.

It's critical to don't forget that stubbornness is a regular part of a toddler's development and may be controlled with persistence, understanding, and regular parenting. If cussed conduct persists and starts offevolved to impact a baby's every day lifestyles, it is able to be useful to trying to find useful useful resource from a pediatrician or intellectual health expert.

Common Traits Of A Stubborn Child

Stubbornness is a commonplace trait amongst kids, and even as it can be frustrating for parents and caregivers, it isn't a terrible first-rate. Stubbornness is usually a signal of a robust-willed infant who's determined to get their manner. However, it's miles essential to apprehend the commonplace trends of a stubborn infant to help them channel their staying electricity and independence in a greater exquisite direction.

Here are a few not unusual developments of a stubborn toddler:

Refusal to Change Their Mind: Stubborn youngsters can be resistant to converting their thoughts, although furnished with new statistics or evidence. They also can dig in their heels and refuse to budge, even though it is smooth that their mind-set is inaccurate.

Strong Opinions: Stubborn youngsters frequently have strong critiques and convictions. They can be captivated with a selected issue matter range or have a sturdy revel in of right and wrong, that could motive them to a lot less probable to compromise.

Persistence: Stubborn kids are continual of their pastimes. They also can maintain to try new subjects or pursue a motive, even within the face of barriers or setbacks.

Independence: Stubborn youngsters frequently have a strong feel of independence and a desire to do matters on their very own. They may additionally withstand assist or guidance from others and prefer to discern matters out on their very private.

Emotional Reactivity: Stubborn children can be emotionally reactive, and may become disillusioned or protecting even as challenged or corrected. They can also furthermore see grievance as a private assault, and respond with anger or defiance.

Understanding those not unusual tendencies of a cussed baby can assist mother and father and caregivers better help and manual them. It is crucial to keep in mind that stubbornness is not a horrific notable, however rather a sign of a baby with a strong will and a desire to say their independence. With patience and know-how, parents and caregivers can help a stubborn little one channel their patience and backbone in a superb path.

Chapter 10: Parenting A Strong-Willed Child

Parenting can be a tough venture, and it may become even more challenging while you are managing a robust-willed infant. A strong-willed little one is character who has a strong revel in of self, is decided, and frequently resists course or authority. While the ones children are regularly perceived as hard to determine, they also can be a supply of exceptional strength and pleasure for his or her parents.

Parenting a strong-willed child calls for a outstanding method than parenting a greater compliant toddler. It requires parents to have patience, knowledge, and the functionality to set clean barriers on the equal time as despite the fact that permitting their little one to say their independence. It can be a balancing act amongst nurturing their infant's independence on the same time as but imparting guidance and help.

In this newsletter, we can explore some of the worrying situations of parenting a sturdy-willed little one, similarly to 3 techniques that could help parents navigate this parenting journey. We may even talk how parents can encourage their child's high-quality capabilities while however helping them to boom electricity of mind and social capabilities. Whether you are a figure of a strong-willed little one or really interested by learning greater approximately this parenting fashion, this newsletter will offer treasured insights into this specific parenting enjoy.

Positive Parenting Techniques

One of existence's maximum tough and enjoyable reports is being a discern. As a decide, your number one motive is to elevate your kids inside the high-quality viable manner, and assist them develop into well-adjusted, assured and sort adults. Positive parenting techniques will let you advantage this purpose.

Positive parenting is an technique to parenting that specializes in building a robust and loving relationship in conjunction with your toddler, at the same time as selling their social, emotional, and cognitive development. This method is based totally mostly on mutual understand, powerful verbal exchange, and trouble-fixing abilties. Positive parenting isn't always about permissive parenting, in which youngsters are allowed to do something they need. It is prepared setting easy obstacles and pointers, and guiding your toddler thru great reinforcement and constructive feedback.

Here are a few awesome parenting techniques that you could adopt to create a healthy and nurturing surroundings in your infant:

1. Build a strong courting along with your toddler: Building a sturdy and loving courting collectively together with your infant is vital for extremely good parenting. Spend exquisite time together along side your toddler, be privy to their dreams and issues, and show them that you care. It is critical to speak correctly together with your toddler, the use of excessive first-class language, and avoiding terrible criticism or sarcasm.

2. Create a exquisite environment: A extraordinary surroundings is vital for your infant's nicely-being. Create a safe and cushty space for your toddler, wherein they will

examine, play, and expand. Encourage immoderate exceptional behaviour, and model powerful behaviour your self. Children study thru instance, so in case you want your toddler to be type, respectful and honest, you want to model those behaviours your self.

three. Use powerful reinforcement: Positive reinforcement is a powerful tool for encouraging wonderful behaviour. Praise your little one once they do something accurate, and feature a very good time their successes. Positive reinforcement can be as easy as announcing "pinnacle pastime" or "properly performed" at the equal time as your little one completes a task or achieves a goal. This will increase their shallowness and encourage them to maintain their powerful behaviour.

4. Encourage independence: Encouraging independence is vital on your toddler's development. Allow your infant to make decisions, and inspire them to take responsibility for their movements. This will help them extend their trouble-solving talents, and boom their self-confidence.

five. Set clear barriers and regulations: Setting clear obstacles and regulations is important for first-rate parenting. Children need form and steering, and clean obstacles and policies offer them with a experience of safety and stability. Explain the guidelines and effects truly, and be regular in implementing them. This will assist your toddler learn how to make proper alternatives and increase electricity of will.

6. Use remarkable region: Positive area is prepared guiding your little one through excellent reinforcement and optimistic remarks, in preference to punishment. Instead of the usage of time-outs or other varieties of punishment, use high fantastic vicinity techniques, along with redirecting your toddler's behaviour, giving them a preference, or providing them a logical final results for his or her moves. This will assist your infant studies from their mistakes and amplify self-law abilities.

7. Foster open verbal exchange: Open verbal exchange is critical for excessive outstanding parenting. Encourage your toddler to precise

their feelings and issues, and concentrate to them without judgment. Use active listening abilties, together with reflecting another time what your infant has stated, to show them which you apprehend and rate their perspective. This will help your toddler make bigger their communication competencies and gather a strong courting with you.

Positive parenting techniques can help you create a healthful and nurturing environment to your little one. Building a robust relationship together along with your little one, growing a superb environment, the usage of amazing reinforcement, encouraging independence, placing easy obstacles and rules, the usage of tremendous discipline, and fostering open conversation are vital for awesome parenting. By adopting those techniques, you can help your infant grow to be a nicely-adjusted, assured, and type grownup.

Strategies For Dealing With Power Struggles

As a determine, it isn't always uncommon to stand strength struggles collectively together with your youngsters. These power struggles can variety from small disagreements over what to consume for dinner to large battles over bedtime sporting activities or show closing dates. No be counted what the problem may be, it's vital to method those situations with staying electricity, statistics, and a willingness to compromise. Here are some techniques for handling power struggles in parenting:

Set easy expectancies and barriers

One of the awesome procedures to save you energy struggles is thru putting easy expectations and barriers collectively together with your youngsters. This method putting in place guidelines and results in advance of time, and speakme them clearly and constantly. When youngsters recognise what is expected of them, they may be tons much less likely to maintain off or check limits.

Stay calm and gathered

When you feel like you're dropping manage of a scenario, it's far important to stay calm and accumulated. Yelling or losing your mood can decorate the scenario and make it extra hard to discover a choice. Take a deep breath, stay composed, and talk calmly and respectfully to your toddler.

Listen to your infant's attitude

It's vital to pay attention in your little one's angle inside the route of a strength warfare. Sometimes children act out due to the reality they will be feeling unheard or misunderstood. Take the time to pay attention to their factor of view and attempt to understand wherein they'll be coming from. This let you discover a compromise that works for each of you.

Offer selections

Offering alternatives can be a effective manner to provide kids a revel in of manage and keep away from strength struggles. For example, in place of telling your infant what to eat for dinner, supply them a few options to select out from. This can assist them feel like they've a say within the do not forget huge range and decrease resistance.

Use exquisite reinforcement

Positive reinforcement can be a effective device for encouraging actual behavior and lowering strength struggles. Praise your toddler once they make particular options and look at the rules, and offer small rewards or incentives for high-quality behavior.

Be normal

Consistency is fundamental on the subject of dealing with strength struggles. Stick for your tips and consequences, and look at via on what you are saying you could do. This can help your infant understand which you suggest what you're announcing and that there are effects for his or her movements.

Seek help at the same time as desired

Parenting is hard paintings, and it is k to are searching out help even as you need it. Talk to buddies, own family contributors, or a therapist if you're struggling with energy struggles or one of a kind parenting disturbing situations. Sometimes getting an outdoor mindset may be useful in finding a choice.

Power struggles are a everyday a part of parenting, however they do not need to be overwhelming. By placing clear expectancies, staying calm, paying attention to your toddler, offering options, the usage of awesome reinforcement, being consistent, and searching out guide at the same time as wanted, you could navigate electricity struggles along side your little one in a healthy and high-quality way. Remember, parenting is a journey, and each undertaking is an opportunity for increase and studying.

Discipline Techniques For Strong-Willed Children

Raising robust-willed kids can be tough, especially as regards to place. These children frequently have a thoughts of their private and aren't afraid to unique their reviews or maintain off closer to authority. However, problem is an essential a part of parenting, and it's far crucial to find out strategies that art work on your toddler's particular character and temperament. Here are some concern strategies for strong-willed children:

Set clean expectancies and boundaries

Strong-willed children thrive on shape and routine. Set smooth expectancies and barriers for his or her behavior, and communicate the ones usually. Let them recognise what's anticipated of them, and what the results may be if they harm the tips. This will help youngsters examine what's and is not suitable.

Offer choices

Strong-willed kids often need to experience like they have got a few control over their lives. Offer them options on every occasion viable, which include what to put on or what to eat for dinner. This can assist them feel like they have got some manipulate over their surroundings, at the equal time as nonetheless retaining limitations and form.

Use superb reinforcement

Positive reinforcement may be a powerful tool in phrases of disciplining sturdy-willed children. Praise them for correct behavior and for following the pointers, and offer small rewards or incentives for first-rate conduct. This can assist them understand that their moves have results, and encourage them to make pinnacle selections.

Give them responsibilities

Strong-willed youngsters frequently thrive once they have duties and duties to complete. Give them age-appropriate obligations to do across the house, which incorporates putting the desk or cleaning up their toys. This can help them sense like they may be contributing to the family, at the same time as furthermore giving them a experience of pleasure and accomplishment.

Use natural consequences

Natural outcomes may be a powerful tool for disciplining robust-willed youngsters. For example, if they do now not want to devour their dinner, they may circulate hungry. If they do not easy up their toys, they may now not be able to play with them the following day. This can help them recognize that their moves have outcomes, without resorting to punishment.

Be consistent

Consistency is high close to disciplining robust-willed kids. Stick on your recommendations and results, and take a look at via on what you are saying you can do. This can assist your infant understand which you imply what you say and that there are effects for their actions.

Practice staying power and empathy

Strong-willed children can be difficult, but it's critical to practice staying strength and empathy at the same time as disciplining them. Try to peer topics from their perspective, and understand that their conduct is often pushed with the useful resource of a preference for manipulate or independence. Respond with love and records, even if they keep off closer to your authority.

Seek useful resource while wanted

Parenting is tough paintings, and it's far okay to are seeking out for help on the identical time as you need it. Talk to distinctive parents or a therapist in case you're suffering to subject your robust-willed little one. Sometimes getting an outdoor perspective can be beneficial in finding a solution that works on your family.

Disciplining strong-willed youngsters can be difficult, but it's miles crucial to find techniques that work on your infant's specific persona and temperament. Set easy expectations and barriers, provide alternatives, use superb reinforcement, deliver them obligations, use natural effects, be steady, workout staying power and empathy, and are seeking out help on the same time as wanted. With persistence and love, you may assist your robust-willed toddler learn how to make pinnacle options and thrive within the global.

Tips For Communicating With Your Child Effectively

Effective communique is crucial for constructing strong relationships with our children. It enables us understand their need and dreams, and allows them experience heard and valued. As mother and father, we need if you need to talk efficiently with our children to assemble be given as genuine with, preserve healthful relationships, and assist them broaden and turn out to be responsible adults. Here are a few suggestions for speakme together with your infant effectively:

Active Listening

Active listening is the inspiration of powerful conversation. Give your undivided hobby to your baby at the same time as they're speaking to you. Make eye contact and avoid distractions like your phone or other devices. Show that you're listening through nodding and acknowledging their terms. Let your little one end their mind in advance than responding.

Use Positive Language

Using extraordinary language can help assemble a excessive fine relationship with your child. Avoid the use of lousy language that may motive them to sense like they may be being scolded or criticized. Instead, use excessive excellent language that boosts immoderate exceptional conduct. For instance, in vicinity of announcing "Stop being lazy and smooth up your room," say "It is probably superb if you could easy up your room in advance than dinner."

Keep an Open Mind

Keeping an open thoughts is important for powerful communique together along with your toddler. Try to apprehend their element of view and why they experience the way they do. Avoid leaping to conclusions or judging them. Listen with an open thoughts, and respond with empathy and information.

Be Honest

Honesty is crucial in constructing don't forget collectively along with your infant. Be sincere with them approximately your mind and emotions, notwithstanding the truth that it is difficult. If you're making a mistake, admit it and express regret. This will show your toddler that it is k to make mistakes and which you're inclined to admit on the identical time as you are wrong.

Avoid Being Judgmental

Avoid being judgmental while speaking together with your toddler. They may not continuously make the first-class alternatives, however it's miles crucial to remember that they're however analyzing and growing. Avoid statements which includes "You need to have identified higher" or "Why did you do this?" Use language that encourages humans to don't forget their movements and examine from their errors as a substitute.

Use Nonverbal Communication

Nonverbal communique, including frame language and tone of voice, can supply greater than phrases on my own. Be aware about your nonverbal cues even as speaking at the facet of your infant. For example, crossing your hands can stumble upon as defensive or closed off. Speaking in a peaceful, reassuring tone can help them feel more comfortable and inspire them to open up.

Use age-suitable language

Using age-suitable language is vital even as speakme along with your infant. Avoid using complex language or ideas that they will now not apprehend. Break down complicated mind into clean terms that they may be able to apprehend. This will help them revel in more assured of their potential to speak with you.

Set Boundaries

Setting boundaries is essential in powerful communique at the side of your toddler. Make it clean what behaviors are right and what outcomes will study within the occasion that they pass those obstacles. This will assist your baby apprehend what is predicted of them and avoid misunderstandings.

Effective verbal exchange is key to constructing strong relationships together together with your infant. Active listening, first rate language, an open thoughts, honesty, nonverbal conversation, age-suitable language, and setting boundaries are all vital components of effective conversation in conjunction with your baby. By going for walks towards the ones strategies, you may construct a sturdy, quality dating together along with your infant and help them broaden and alternate into accountable adults.

Building A Strong Relationship With Your Child

One of life's most fun opinions is being a discern. Watching your little one grow and change into their own precise character is a supply of notable delight for any parent. However, raising a toddler is not an smooth mission, and it calls for pretty some time, effort, and patience. Building a sturdy dating along with your infant is one of the most crucial components of parenting. A strong relationship assist you to guide your infant thru the traumatic situations of life and create a bond to be able to ultimate an entire life.

Here are some hints for constructing a strong relationship together along with your little one in parenting:

1. Spend Quality Time Together

Spending quality time together collectively along with your toddler is one of the first-class techniques to assemble a sturdy dating. Quality time way placing aside time to attention in your child with none distractions. This can be something from studying a e book collectively, going for a stroll, or genuinely sitting right down to have a communication. The secret's to ensure that your infant feels valued and desired.

2. Listen to Your Child

Listening for your toddler is an essential a part of building a strong courting. Children want to experience heard and understood. When your toddler speaks, pay interest attentively, and try to apprehend their point of view. This will help them experience mounted and respected, and it will furthermore assist you recognize their goals and issues.

three. Show Empathy

Empathy is the capability to understand and percent every different man or woman's emotions. As a determine, it is vital to reveal empathy inside the course of your infant. This method acknowledging their emotions and feelings and displaying them that you care. Empathy permits assemble take into account and creates a regular place in your little one to open up and percentage their thoughts and emotions.

four. Set Boundaries

Setting barriers is an vital a part of building a sturdy courting in conjunction with your toddler. Boundaries help your infant apprehend what is anticipated of them and what isn't allowed. They additionally assist your little one boom a revel in of responsibility and duty. However, it's far critical to keep in mind that boundaries need to be set in a loving and respectful manner.

five. Be a Role Model

Children have a study via manner of example, and as a parent, you are their maximum sizeable characteristic version. It's vital to manual thru example and version the behaviors you need to peer for your toddler. This manner working towards top conduct which includes honesty, recognize, and kindness. When your toddler sees you modeling those behaviors, they may be much more likely to undertake them themselves.

6. Practice Positive Reinforcement

Positive reinforcement is a effective device for constructing a sturdy relationship together collectively with your infant. This way praising your toddler for their correct conduct and efforts. Positive reinforcement facilitates build shallowness and encourages your infant to maintain to make nice selections.

7. Keep Communication Open

Open communique is essential to building a robust relationship together with your toddler. Make sure your infant knows they may be able to come to you with any questions or worries they may have. Encourage open and honest conversation thru listening without judgment and being supportive.

eight. Be Patient

Building a sturdy courting collectively with your infant takes time and staying power. It is important to live persistent and affected individual on your efforts. Remember that constructing a robust dating is a lifelong machine, and it requires ongoing attempt.

Building a sturdy dating together along with your infant is one of the most important elements of parenting. Spending excellent time collectively, paying attention to your child, showing empathy, setting boundaries, being a characteristic version, working towards brilliant reinforcement, maintaining conversation open, and being affected character are all key components of building a sturdy relationship. By following the ones pointers, you could create a bond together with your toddler as a manner to very last a whole lifestyles.

Chapter 11: Dealing With Aggressive, Defiant And Disobedient Children

As a decide or caregiver, coping with competitive, defiant, and disobedient kids may be one of the maximum tough and stressful stories. Children can display a whole lot of behaviors that may be difficult to manipulate, which includes tantrums, yelling, hitting, biting, and refusing to have a observe hints or commands. These behaviors may be tense and hard for dad and mom and caregivers, and may have a negative impact at the complete circle of relatives.

It is vital to understand that youngsters also can show off those behaviors for loads of reasons. Some kids can be struggling with emotional or behavioral problems, at the same time as others can be reacting to stress or modifications of their surroundings. Regardless of the cause, it is critical to address those behaviors in a excessive high-quality and excessive remarkable manner, at the same time as additionally putting easy barriers and expectancies for youngsters.

Dealing with competitive, defiant, and disobedient youngsters requires patience, consistency, and a willingness to comply to taken into consideration one of a type situations. Parents and caregivers want to be inclined to be aware of their kids, understand their attitude, and offer them with the assist and steerage they want to amplify appropriate coping techniques and conduct patterns.

There are many techniques and techniques that dad and mom and caregivers can use to help control and decrease aggressive, defiant, and disobedient behaviors in youngsters. These may also moreover include placing easy policies and outcomes, using first-rate reinforcement and praise, providing shape and routine, and looking for professional assist and steering even as important.

It is critical to consider that parenting is a gaining knowledge of machine, and no man or woman has all the solutions. However, by running together with kids, supplying them with the help and guidance they need, and the use of a whole lot of techniques and strategies, mother and father and caregivers can assist their kids discover ways to control their feelings, enlarge excessive great behaviors, and collect healthful relationships with others.

Understanding The Root Causes Of Aggressive Behavior

Aggressive behavior in kids is a not unusual and tough trouble that mother and father and caregivers regularly come across. Children may additionally show various forms of aggressive behaviors together with hitting, biting, pushing, and yelling, that may purpose damage to others and themselves. Understanding the muse causes of aggressive behavior in youngsters is essential to successfully address the difficulty and prevent it from escalating.

There are different factors that could contribute to competitive behavior in kids. Some of the most commonplace root reasons are discussed beneath:

Biological factors

Biological elements which include genetics, mind chemistry, and hormonal imbalances should have an effect on a infant's conduct. Children who have a family records of aggression or highbrow health problems are more likely to expose off aggressive behaviors. Moreover, positive scientific situations which includes ADHD, autism, and conduct sickness also can make a contribution to aggressive behavior in children.

Environmental factors

Environmental factors collectively with parenting style, circle of relatives dynamics, and exposure to violence should have an impact on a toddler's behavior. Children who broaden up in families with plenty of war, aggression, or violence also can growth competitive behaviors as a manner to manage or defend themselves. Similarly, children who're exposed to violence of their network or media may additionally grow to be desensitized to it and normalize competitive conduct.

Lack of social competencies

Children who lack social talents together with communique, problem-solving, and self-law may additionally additionally inn to aggressive behaviors once they stumble upon tough conditions or conflicts with others. These children also can have problem expressing their feelings or wishes, and won't apprehend the way to solve conflicts in a non-violent way.

Trauma and strain

Traumatic tales collectively with abuse, neglect, or witnessing violence can have a profound effect on a infant's conduct. Children who've experienced trauma may additionally additionally have hassle regulating their emotions, and might show off competitive behaviors as a manner to cope with their emotions of fear, anger, or unhappiness. Moreover, kids who experience continual pressure which consist of poverty, instability, or parental struggle can also be at hazard for growing aggressive behaviors.

Modeling

Children take a look at with the resource of watching the behavior of others, mainly their dad and mom and caregivers. If a infant sees adults using aggressive behavior to resolve problems or specific their feelings, they'll adopt comparable behaviors. Similarly, publicity to violent media collectively with video video video games or movies also can have an impact on a little one's behavior.

Understanding the concept reasons of aggressive conduct in youngsters is the first step in addressing the problem. Parents and caregivers can take numerous steps to assist their children enlarge best and non-violent methods of expressing themselves and resolving conflicts. These steps might also moreover embody looking for expert help which includes remedy or counseling, presenting a stable and solid environment, coaching social talents, and modeling nice behaviors. With staying power, consistency, and assist, kids can discover ways to control their feelings and precise themselves in wholesome and optimistic strategies.

Techniques For Dealing With Defiant And Disobedient Behavior

Parenting may be a difficult system, and one of the most hard elements is handling defiant and disobedient behavior in children. Whether it is a toddler throwing a tantrum, a college-age toddler refusing to do homework, or a teenager breaking guidelines, defiant conduct can be traumatic, difficult, or perhaps infuriating for dad and mom. However, there are techniques and strategies that parents can use to control defiant and disobedient conduct of their kids.

Stay Calm and Consistent:

It is crucial to stay calm and composed whilst handling defiant and disobedient conduct in children. When mother and father lose their cool and react in anger or frustration, it often makes the situation worse. Instead, dad and mom should stay calm, use a relaxed voice, and avoid yelling or harsh punishments. Parents have to additionally be consistent of their responses to disobedient behavior, ensuring to set clean expectancies and results and following via with them commonly.

Use Positive Reinforcement:

Positive reinforcement is a effective device for shaping behavior in children. Parents can use powerful reinforcement to inspire correct behavior and discourage disobedience. For instance, dad and mom can praise their infant for completing a venture or following a rule or provide a small reward for correctly behavior. Positive reinforcement may be specially effective for greater youthful kids who won't recognize the outcomes of their movements.

Set Clear Expectations and Consequences:

One of the keys to handling defiant conduct is putting smooth expectations and consequences. Parents need to be clear approximately what conduct is anticipated in their youngsters and what consequences will quit give up end result from disobedience. It is important to be regular in enforcing results and to make certain they may be appropriate for the behavior in query. Parents have to furthermore make certain their infant is aware of why the outcomes are being imposed and what behavior is predicted within the destiny.

Empathize and Listen:

It may be clean to get caught up in our non-public frustration and anger at the same time as managing defiant behavior. However, taking the time to pay interest on your toddler and empathize with their feelings can be a effective manner to defuse the situation. By acknowledging your little one's feelings and mindset, you may assist them sense heard and understood, that could reason them to more inclined to cooperate and check pointers.

Offer Choices:

Giving children a feel of control and desire may be an effective way to inspire cooperation and discourage defiant conduct. Parents can offer selections in regions in which it is suitable, along with permitting a little one to select what they want to vicinity on or what activity they need to do. However, it's far critical to offer choices in the context of easy expectancies and consequences.

Seek Professional Help:

If defiant behavior is chronic and intense, it can be essential to are searching for expert help. A highbrow health expert can help dad and mom and children increase strategies for coping with defiant behavior and cope with any underlying problems that may be contributing to the conduct.

Dealing with defiant and disobedient conduct in kids can be a venture, but it isn't always no longer feasible. By staying calm and steady, the use of awesome reinforcement, putting clean expectancies and effects, empathizing and listening, offering alternatives, and trying to find professional assist at the same time as vital, mother and father can control defiant behavior and assist their youngsters expand nice, cooperative behaviors.

Strategies For Managing Tantrums And Meltdowns

Tantrums and meltdowns are a common prevalence in parenting, especially inside the route of the early years of a infant's development. They can be irritating and difficult for parents, however there are techniques which could assist manage those hard behaviors.

Stay Calm and Patient:

When a toddler is having a tantrum or meltdown, it is able to be smooth for mother and father to come to be annoyed, angry, or beaten. However, it's far vital to live calm and affected man or woman. Yelling, scolding, or punishing a baby all through a tantrum or meltdown could make the scenario worse. Instead, take deep breaths, stay calm, and try to live focused on resolving the problem available.

Offer Comfort and Support:

Tantrums and meltdowns can be distressing for children, and they may be feeling overwhelmed or upset. Offering comfort and assist can help to assuage and calm the child. This may also contain maintaining the kid, the usage of a calming voice, or supplying a fave toy or blanket. Sometimes, all a toddler desires is to sense that someone is there for them.

Identify and Address Triggers:

Tantrums and meltdowns frequently have triggers, together with hunger, fatigue, or frustration. By identifying and addressing the ones triggers, dad and mom can assist save you destiny outbursts. For example, if a little one frequently has a tantrum at the identical time as they may be hungry, make sure they have got normal snacks or food. If a little one has hassle transitioning from one hobby to some different, provide them a caution in advance and offer a countdown.

Use Distractions and Redirection:

Sometimes, it is useful to distract or redirect a little one who is having a tantrum or meltdown. This may be completed thru offering a completely unique hobby or toy, or by means of using appealing the child in a special conversation or topic. For instance, if a toddler is upset because they cannot have a particular toy, offer them a awesome toy to play with or advise a one-of-a-kind hobby.

Use Positive Reinforcement:

Positive reinforcement is a effective device for managing tantrums and meltdowns. By profitable precise conduct, dad and mom can inspire kids to maintain behaving surely. This may additionally moreover include supplying reward, hugs, or a small reward for particular behavior. Positive reinforcement can assist to create a fine and supportive environment for the child.

Teach Coping Skills:

Teaching children coping capabilities may be beneficial in managing tantrums and meltdowns. This can encompass schooling children a way to particular their feelings in a wholesome way, deep respiration strategies, or a way to trouble-remedy. By giving youngsters the equipment to govern their feelings, dad and mom can help to lessen the frequency and depth of tantrums and meltdowns.

Tantrums and meltdowns can be tough for mother and father, but there are techniques which could assist control those behaviors. By staying calm and affected person, supplying comfort and manual, figuring out and addressing triggers, the use of distractions and redirection, using first-rate reinforcement, and education coping abilties, parents can create a remarkable and supportive environment for their kids to thrive in.

Helping Your Child Cope With Anger And Frustration

Anger and frustration are herbal feelings that kids revel in as they develop and broaden. As a determine, it's far important to assist your infant discover ways to address these emotions in a healthy and best manner. Here are some strategies you may use to help your little one manage their anger and frustration:

Model Healthy Coping Skills:

Children have a look at thru gazing their mother and father, so it's far essential to version healthful coping skills in your little one. When you sense angry or irritated, take a 2nd to pause and take some deep breaths. Talk on your infant about how you experience and what you're doing to govern your emotions. This will help your infant see that it is ordinary to sense indignant or aggravated, and that there are healthful techniques to deal with these feelings.

Help Your Child Identify Their Emotions:

Sometimes kids won't understand the way to turn out to be aware about and explicit their emotions. Encourage your toddler to name their emotions and speak about what they're feeling. This will assist them come to be extra aware about their emotions and increase the capacity to specific them in a healthy way.

Teach Problem-Solving Skills:

When your child is feeling indignant or annoyed, help them apprehend the trouble and art work through viable answers. This will assist them expand hassle-fixing abilties that they may use in distinctive regions of their existence. Encourage your toddler to brainstorm certainly one of a type answers and examine the professionals and cons of each choice.

Encourage Physical Activity:

Physical hobby can be a tremendous manner for children to launch pent-up strength and emotions. Encourage your infant to interact in physical sports activities sports that they enjoy, along with playing out of doors, going for a walk, or playing a recreation.

Teach Relaxation Techniques:

Teaching your infant rest techniques, together with deep respiration, can assist them loosen up even as they're feeling irritated or annoyed. Encourage your toddler to take deep breaths and remember to ten while they will be feeling dissatisfied.

Provide Positive Reinforcement:

When your toddler is able to deal with their emotions in a wholesome manner, provide notable reinforcement by way of the use of manner of praising and acknowledging their efforts. This will assist them enjoy recommended and brought directly to keep the usage of healthful coping abilities.

Helping your toddler address anger and frustration is an important a part of parenting. By modeling wholesome coping abilties, helping your little one pick out their emotions, teaching hassle-fixing talents, encouraging physical pastime, teaching relaxation techniques, and presenting great reinforcement, you could help your little one enlarge the abilties they need to control their feelings in a wholesome and extremely good manner.

Chapter 12: Parenting Skills

Parenting capabilities communicate over with the skills, attitudes, and behaviors that parents use to engage with and lift their youngsters. Effective parenting abilties incorporate creating a nurturing and supportive environment that fosters the bodily, emotional, and social development of kids. The characteristic of dad and mom in a little one's existence is crucial, as they may be the number one caregivers and the number one teachers. Parenting competencies are observed through enjoy, assertion, and schooling, and they play a important characteristic in shaping a toddler's man or woman, values, and future success. The manner parents interact with their youngsters should have a excellent effect on their highbrow health, educational success, and social relationships. This is why it's far crucial for dad and mom to enlarge and exercise powerful parenting talents a good way to help them create a outstanding and supportive environment for their kids to thrive in. In this text, we are able to discuss a few important parenting abilties that every determine must recognize to assist them enhance happy, healthful, and properly-adjusted children.

Developing Good Communication Skills

Parenting is one of the maximum hard but profitable roles in life. As a figure, it's far important to amplify well verbal exchange competencies to preserve a wholesome dating on the facet of your infant. Effective verbal exchange skills will can help you understand your infant's mind, feelings, and goals, and could allow you to reply in a supportive and empathetic way. Here are a few tips on developing top conversation capabilities in parenting:

1. Listen actively: Listening is the inspiration of excellent conversation. Active listening consists of taking note of what your infant is announcing and responding in a way that indicates you recognize and care approximately their thoughts and emotions. It is important to offer your toddler your undivided hobby while they're speakme and avoid interrupting or brushing off their worries.

2. Be smooth and concise: When communicating along with your infant, it is crucial to be clean and concise in your message. Use clean language and avoid the usage of complicated vocabulary or prolonged sentences that might confuse your little one. Make pleasant your infant is aware of what you're announcing, and ask them to copy lower lower back what they heard to make certain clean conversation.

3. Use wonderful language: Positive language can assist create a supportive and nurturing surroundings. Instead of criticizing or blaming your infant, use first-rate language to inspire precise behavior and support super inclinations. For example, in place of saying "You're lazy," say "I comprehend you are able to doing first rate matters, permit's art work on getting began."

four. Validate your infant's feelings: It is essential to famend and validate your infant's emotions. Let your toddler recognize that it's far k to experience a excellent manner and that their feelings are crucial. When your toddler stocks their feelings with you, keep away from brushing off or ignoring them, and rather reply with empathy and records.

five. Use nonverbal conversation: Nonverbal communique, along side facial expressions and frame language, can play a giant role in verbal exchange. Pay hobby on your very very personal nonverbal cues, as they are capable of supply a message on your toddler. For instance, a smile can advocate approval and encouragement, whilst a frown can imply unhappiness or disapproval.

6. Show respect: Respect is crucial in any relationship, which incorporates the determine-infant courting. Treat your toddler with appreciate through listening to their critiques, displaying hobby in their sports activities, and averting judgment or grievance. When you show recognize to your little one, they'll be much more likely to accept as genuine with and open up to you.

Developing actual verbal exchange skills in parenting is important to hold a wholesome and excessive first-class relationship together in conjunction with your child. Active listening, using tremendous language, validating your toddler's emotions, the use of nonverbal communique, and displaying recognize allow you to speak successfully together together with your toddler and foster a supportive and nurturing environment.

Setting Boundaries And Rules

As a determine, placing obstacles and regulations is an important part of developing a secure and nurturing environment on your infant. Rules offer shape and consistency, and boundaries assist your infant apprehend what is predicted of them and what isn't always relevant behavior. Here are a few pointers on placing barriers and policies in parenting:

Be smooth and ordinary: When placing regulations and barriers, be clean about your expectancies and communicate them continually. Make superb your infant is familiar with the results of breaking the regulations, and put in force them usually.

Involve your baby: Involve your infant in setting the hints and obstacles, especially as they grow antique. This can assist your little one revel in greater invested inside the gadget and much more likely to comply with the regulations. Allow them to offer guidelines and offer feedback, and be open to compromise.

Prioritize protection: Safety have to be a pinnacle precedence whilst placing tips and boundaries. Establish protection policies, which incorporates sporting a helmet at the same time as using a bike or now not talking to strangers, and make sure your infant is aware of the importance of following them.

Be age-appropriate: Rules and obstacles need to be age-suitable and keep in mind your little one's developmental level. Young youngsters may moreover furthermore need extra guidance and structure, on the equal time as older kids may additionally moreover gain from extra independence and flexibility.

Be bendy: While consistency is essential, it is also vital to be bendy and adapt policies as your little one grows and develops. Revisit hints periodically and make adjustments as needed to reflect your little one's converting desires and abilties.

Use fantastic reinforcement: Positive reinforcement, which consist of praise or rewards, can be an effective way to inspire your little one to take a look at the rules. When your little one follows the tips, reward them and allow them to understand you recognize their accurate behavior.

Setting barriers and recommendations is an important part of parenting. Being smooth and regular, concerning your little one, prioritizing safety, being age-appropriate, being bendy, and using outstanding reinforcement can help you set obstacles and tips in parenting.

Providing Structure And Routine

Providing form and recurring is an vital detail of parenting which can have a large impact on a little one's development and properly-being. When kids understand what to anticipate and characteristic a ordinary routine, they feel more solid and can higher manipulate their feelings and behaviors. In this newsletter, we can talk the significance of supplying shape and regular in parenting and the manner to put into effect it efficiently.

Why is supplying shape and routine crucial in parenting?

Children thrive in a established surroundings wherein they sense solid and solid. Providing shape and routine permits children boom a revel in of predictability and order, that can lessen anxiety and pressure. Additionally, having a ordinary ordinary can help kids take a look at vital existence capabilities collectively with time manipulate, commercial enterprise organization, and duty.

Structure and routine can also offer a experience of balance at some point of instances of change or transition, collectively with transferring to a state-of-the-art home, starting faculty, or the transport of a extremely-contemporary sibling. Having a regular recurring can help youngsters alter to those modifications extra resultseasily.

How to position into effect form and routine in parenting?

1. Implementing shape and everyday in parenting requires a deliberate and intentional method. Here are a few strategies for offering form and habitual in parenting:

2. Set a normal every day normal: Establish a consistent every day ordinary to your toddler, collectively with ordinary instances for waking up, meals, homework, playtime, and bedtime.

three. Be smooth and regular: Be easy in conjunction with your expectancies and constantly enforce the regulations and outcomes. Children want clean limitations to feel steady and constant.

4. Use visible aids: Visual aids together with charts or schedules may be useful in establishing a ordinary and speaking expectations to kids.

5. Encourage independence: Encourage your infant to take obligation for their every day habitual through associated with them in

selection-making and allowing them to take possession in their time table.

6. Be bendy: While recurring and shape are important, it is also vital to be flexible and adaptable even as important. Unexpected events may additionally furthermore disrupt your time table, so be prepared to modify as wanted.

7. Model the behavior you want to look: Children study thru example, so model the conduct you want to see in your toddler. If you need your infant to be prepared, punctual, and accountable, then monitor the ones characteristics your self.

Providing form and normal in parenting is critical for kid's emotional and behavioral nicely-being. Implementing a everyday everyday calls for planned effort and intentionality, but the advantages are clearly nicely worth it. With a hooked up and predictable surroundings, youngsters can amplify important existence abilities and sense safe and steady, that may set them up for fulfillment in the future.

Nurturing Your Child's Emotional Well-Being

Nurturing your little one's emotional nicely-being is vital for his or her everyday improvement and success in lifestyles. Here are some recommendations that will help you useful resource your infant's emotional health:

Create a stable and loving surroundings: Children thrive in an environment wherein they experience consistent, cherished, and supported. Provide a regular and predictable ordinary, specific your love and affection often, and find time for high-quality one-on-one time at the side of your infant.

Listen and validate their feelings: It's critical to pay interest to your infant and famend their feelings, even in case you do no longer normally recall them. Validating their feelings lets in your child experience heard and understood.

Teach emotional law: Help your toddler discover ways to apprehend and manipulate their feelings. Encourage them to particular their emotions in healthful strategies and train them strategies which incorporates deep respiration or taking a harm to loosen up.

Encourage incredible self-talk: Help your little one make bigger a awesome self-picture through encouraging excellent self-speak. Teach them to consciousness on their strengths and to be kind to themselves.

Model wholesome emotional behavior: Children observe thru example, so it is important to version healthful emotional behavior. Show your toddler the manner to cope with pressure, explicit feelings correctly, and treatment conflicts in a tremendous way.

Foster wonderful relationships: Strong relationships with circle of relatives and friends can provide a assist device for your infant. Encourage pleasant relationships by means of putting in playdates, taking element in sports together, and modeling healthful relationships yourself.

Seek assist if desired: If you're worried approximately your toddler's emotional nicely-being, do no longer hesitate to attempting to find professional help. A intellectual fitness professional can provide guidance and manual to your infant and your own family.

Help them growth a growth mindset: Encourage your child to embody stressful conditions and errors as opportunities to analyze and develop. Teach them that failure is a natural a part of the studying technique and that they're succesful to triumph over boundaries with attempt and perseverance.

Limit publicity to poor media: Be aware of the media your infant is uncovered to, as bad snap shots and messages can impact their emotional nicely-being. Limit their publicity to violent or beside the factor content fabric and have open conversations with them about what they see.

Encourage healthful conduct: Physical health is mounted to emotional well-being, so inspire your child to adopt wholesome habits which include everyday workout, healthy eating, and getting sufficient sleep.

Celebrate their achievements: Recognize and rejoice your little one's accomplishments, regardless of how small. Positive reinforcement can enhance their vanity and inspire them to hold to work in the path in their goals.

Practice gratitude: Help your infant boom an mind-set of gratitude via using encouraging them to interest at the wonderful additives of their life. Have them maintain a gratitude journal or make it a each day exercise to share subjects they're grateful for.

By nurturing your infant's emotional properly-being, you are setting them up for a wholesome and a success future. Remember to be affected person, kind, and supportive as your baby navigates the u.S.And downs of life.

Chapter 13: Child Care

Child care is a crucial carrier that gives care and supervision for more youthful kids on the identical time as their mother and father or caregivers are away. Child care can take many bureaucracy, from in-home care through a nanny or babysitter to formal care provided through certified little one care centers or family little one care houses. The significance of little one care can't be overstated, as it performs a vital characteristic in supporting the wholesome development of younger youngsters, allowing mother and father to artwork or attend college, and contributing to the general properly-being of families and businesses.

Quality infant care not remarkable offers a steady and nurturing surroundings for kids but also promotes their social, emotional, cognitive, and bodily development. It also can assist youngsters construct excessive pleasant relationships with pals and adults, increase important skills and expertise, and put together them for success in college and past. For parents and caregivers, notable baby care can provide peace of thoughts, help art work-circle of relatives stability, and decorate their children's gaining knowledge of and development.

However, having access to top notch little one care can be a huge task for loads families because of various factors which includes rate, availability, and brilliant. Therefore, policymakers, educators, and advocates have to art work together to make sure that all households have get proper of get entry to to to lots less high priced, extremely good baby care that meets their dreams and promotes the wholesome improvement of younger youngsters.

Importance Of Quality Child Care

Quality baby care is critical for parents who want to balance paintings and own family obligations. As a determine, presenting your infant with super little one care could have severa advantages for each you and your infant.

Firstly, amazing infant care offers a steady and nurturing environment for youngsters to observe and make bigger. Children who collect first-rate infant care are much more likely to have splendid tales with caregivers and exclusive children, that can sell social and emotional improvement. In addition, super baby care can offer kids with opportunities to have a examine new capabilities and understanding, together with language, math, technological know-how, and social skills, that might assist them attain college and past.

Secondly, brilliant little one care can help mother and father enjoy regular and confident in their choice of deal with their kids. When dad and mom realize their children are receiving incredible care, they're able to cognizance on their art work or precise duties with out annoying approximately their children's safety or nicely-being. This can lessen stress and anxiety and beautify regular own family properly-being.

Thirdly, best toddler care can manual excellent parent-infant relationships. When children get hold of excellent infant care, they will develop robust relationships with their caregivers, which can assist them revel in extra sturdy and assured. As a end result, parents may additionally additionally sense greater linked to their children and additional confident of their parenting competencies.

Finally, amazing infant care can beneficial useful resource parents' profession and education dreams. When mother and father have get right of access to to first-rate little one care, they're able to hold to art work or attend college on the equal time as understanding that their children are steady and properly cared for. This can decorate financial stability and provide possibilities for parents to beautify their careers or training.

Quality toddler care is an crucial trouble of parenting. It gives youngsters with a steady and nurturing surroundings to observe and boom, enables excellent determine-infant relationships, and allows parents to stability art work and circle of relatives responsibilities. Investing in exceptional little one care can gain every mother and father and children and make contributions to the overall nicely-being of families and groups.

Choosing The Right Child Care Provider

Choosing the proper little one care company in your toddler is an essential selection that can have a widespread impact in your little one's development and nicely-being. Here are a few hints to help you select the right toddler care issuer:

1. Determine your little one's desires: Before you start looking for toddler care companies, decide what your little one's goals are. Consider their age, temperament, and any specific needs they may have.

2. Consider your options: There are numerous forms of little one care companies available, which incorporates daycare facilities, circle of relatives child care homes, and in-home caregivers. Research each preference to decide which one is tremendous to your toddler and family.

three. Research companies: Once you've got identified capability toddler care carriers, do some studies to learn more about them. Check their licensing and accreditation reputation, observe critiques, and ask for references.

four. Visit the power: Schedule a visit to the child care facility to check the environment and meet the frame of human beings. Pay hobby to how the caregivers engage with the children, and make sure that the facility is straightforward, stable, and nicely-maintained.

five. Ask questions: During your visit, ask the caregivers and frame of employees any questions you may have about their guidelines, processes, and curriculum. Ask approximately their experience and education, as well as how they deal with disciplinary problems and emergencies.

6. Trust your instincts: Ultimately, believe your instincts even as selecting a child care business enterprise. If something couldn't revel in proper or you have were given concerns, it can be outstanding to preserve your are seeking out till you discover a issuer that meets your needs and appears like a outstanding in form to your own family.

Remember, deciding on the proper infant care agency is a important choice that could have a big effect to your little one's development and well-being. Take the time to do your research, ask questions, and take delivery of as real together with your instincts to make sure that you discover the wonderful organisation in your little one and own family.

Tips For Finding Affordable Child Care Options

Finding low-fee little one care can be a primary mission for plenty dad and mom. However, with some cautious planning and studies, it's far possible to find out low-charge infant care options that meet your own family's desires. Here are a few recommendations for locating a lot less highly-priced infant care alternatives:

1. Consider circle of relatives and buddies: One of the maximum reasonably-priced baby care options is to invite circle of relatives or friends to observe your baby. This may be especially useful in case you most effective need occasional infant care.

2. Check on the facet of your company: Some employers provide on-site baby care or have partnerships with nearby infant care corporations, which can be a more inexpensive opportunity than one of a kind agencies within the region.

3. Look for authorities-funded packages: There are several authorities-funded little one care applications that offer less costly infant care alternatives for low-earnings families. These programs may also moreover have earnings and eligibility requirements, so it is important to test if you qualify.

four. Research community little one care providers: Look for infant care vendors on your area and evaluate prices. You might also additionally discover that a few corporations are greater less expensive than others, and may provide reductions for siblings or longer hours.

five. Consider in-domestic toddler care: In-domestic infant care carriers may be extra cheap than daycare facilities, and can provide more flexibility with hours and offerings.

6. Look for baby care co-ops: Child care co-ops are companies of parents who take turns looking each awesome's children. This can be a more inexpensive alternative, as mother and father take turns looking the youngsters without figuring out to buy little one care.

7. Ask approximately economic assistance: Some infant care businesses provide economic help applications for households who want assist buying little one care. It's properly nicely really worth asking if that is an opportunity for you.

8. Plan beforehand: Planning beforehand will can help you locate more cheaper toddler care options. Start searching out infant care providers as quickly as viable, and recollect issue-time or bendy schedules to save cash.

By following these tips, you can discover low-cost little one care options that meet your family's dreams. Remember to don't forget all your options, and to ask for help and manual even as you want it.

Chapter 14: Imparting Moral Education To Kids

Imparting moral training to kids is an crucial problem of parenting. It consists of coaching children about right and wrong, instilling values inclusive of honesty, empathy, and apprehend, and growing their person.

Moral training begins at home, wherein parents play a vital feature in shaping their toddler's ideals and values. Parents can begin with the aid of placing precise examples and being incredible characteristic fashions for his or her children. They can train children to be kind, respectful, and compassionate closer to others and the surroundings.

Parents can use severa techniques to impart moral training to their kids, collectively with storytelling, discussing ethical dilemmas, and the usage of actual-lifestyles examples. They can also contain youngsters in network provider and volunteering activities, which assist them extend empathy and compassion.

Moral education is an ongoing manner that requires staying strength, consistency, and open communication. Parents must inspire their kids to invite questions, precise their critiques, and take part in discussions to assist them broaden critical wondering abilities and a feel of responsibility.

Imparting moral schooling to kids is an critical part of parenting, and it permits kids emerge as responsible, compassionate, and ethical adults.

The Importance Of Teaching Moral Values To Children

Teaching moral values to youngsters is an essential trouble of parenting. It allows children broaden a strong experience of right and incorrect, make moral selections, and construct man or woman. Here are some of the motives why education ethical values to children is crucial:

1. Helps increase empathy and compassion: By education ethical values which consist of kindness, apprehend, and empathy, dad and mom can assist children learn how to recognize and take care of others. These values help children boom healthful relationships, assemble

strong connections with others, and create a pleasant impact in their communities.

2. Helps children make better picks: When children take a look at moral values, they emerge as extra privy to their movements and the impact they have on others. This consciousness lets in kids make higher decisions that align with their values and ideals.

3. Builds resilience: Teaching moral values which embody perseverance, honesty, and duty permits children boom resilience. They learn how to deal with stressful conditions and setbacks, and boom a sense of willpower that facilitates them overcome boundaries and accumulate their dreams.

4. Prepares youngsters for the future: In contemporary international, it's miles essential for youngsters to have a robust experience of ethics and values. By coaching them moral values, mother and father can prepare their children for the stressful situations they'll face inside the destiny and help them become responsible and a success adults.

5. Promotes a incredible society: When kids have a look at ethical values, they grow to be accountable residents who contribute to society. They are much more likely to make excellent contributions to their companies and create a higher worldwide for every body.

Teaching ethical values to kids is essential for their non-public and social development. Parents play a essential position in instilling the ones values in their children, and it allows them turn out to be responsible, compassionate, and ethical people.

Ways To Teach Moral Values To Children

Teaching ethical values to kids is an essential thing of parenting. Here are a few techniques to teach ethical values to youngsters:

1. Be a function model: Children observe with the useful resource of searching their parents, so it's far vital to model the moral values which you want your kids to analyze. For example, in case you want your infant to be sincere, you need to constantly inform the reality.

2. Talk about values: Have regular conversations together with your toddler approximately moral values which include appreciate, kindness, honesty, and duty. Use real-life examples to illustrate the importance of those values.

3. Read reminiscences: Reading stories that teach moral instructions is an powerful way to help children apprehend moral values. You can find many books that train moral lessons for children.

4. Use high first-class reinforcement: When your infant shows a moral price, reward them and reward them for their behavior. This will inspire them to keep to reveal great conduct.

five. Set easy expectations: Set clear expectations on your infant's conduct and supply an purpose of why it's far important to test those pointers.

6. Encourage empathy: Encourage your toddler to bear in mind distinctive human beings's emotions and perspectives. This will assist them growth empathy and recognize the

significance of treating others with kindness and understand.

7. Provide opportunities for volunteering: Volunteering is an first-rate manner to teach children the importance of supporting others and being responsible citizens. Look for volunteer possibilities for your network that your toddler can take part in.

Overall, coaching ethical values to children requires staying energy, consistency, and a willpower to being a wonderful position version. By the usage of those strategies, you could assist your little one enlarge a strong ethical foundation in order to serve them nicely at some point of their lives.

Tips For Imparting Moral Education With Love And Grace

Here are a few tips for imparting ethical education with love and fashion in parenting:

1. Build a strong courting together with your toddler: Children are much more likely to pay attention and follow their dad and mom' moral teachings once they enjoy cherished and

related to them. Spend nice time along with your child, pay attention to them, and show them affection.

2. Use notable language: When speaking to your toddler about moral values, use awesome language rather than awful language. For instance, in place of announcing, "Don't be rude," say, "Be kind to others."

three. Practice staying power: Teaching ethical values is a protracted-time period system, and it calls for patience. Do now not expect your toddler to have a look at and take a look at everything right now. Instead, hobby on incremental development and praise your little one's efforts.

four. Show empathy and understanding: Children may also moreover make errors or behave in methods that pass closer to the ethical values you are trying to educate. Show empathy and information, and use the ones situations as teachable moments.

5. Use recollections and examples: Children observe via recollections and examples. Use

age-appropriate memories and actual-lifestyles examples to demonstrate the importance of ethical values.

6. Encourage crucial wondering: Encourage your toddler to assume drastically and ask questions about moral values. Help them apprehend the reasoning behind the values and the manner they study in unique situations.

7. Be consistent: Consistency is crucial whilst teaching moral values. Stick to the values you educate and study them commonly on your private behavior.

eight. Use herbal consequences: Instead of the usage of punishment, use natural results to help your little one apprehend the effect of their movements on others and the sector spherical them.

Overall, offering moral training with love and attraction requires a deep records of your child's wishes and talents, staying power, consistency, and a strength of mind to great parenting. By the usage of these recommendations, you could create a loving and supportive surroundings that lets in your infant broaden sturdy ethical values.

Chapter 15: Definition Of Positive Parenting

Positive parenting is an approach to parenting that emphasizes effective reinforcement, open communique, and problem-fixing talents to beautify high excellent conduct in kids, in choice to counting on punishment or horrible reinforcement. The purpose of excessive excellent parenting is to construct a robust, healthy dating amongst discern and infant, at the same time as coaching kids vital existence competencies and helping them expand a fantastic self-picture. Positive parenting techniques incorporate growing a nurturing and supportive surroundings, setting clean and normal limits, the usage of herbal effects, and galvanizing problem-fixing and creativity in youngsters. By that specialize in first-rate reinforcement and verbal exchange, excessive quality parenting allows parents growth assured, resilient, and nicely-adjusted youngsters.

WHY POSITIVE PARENTING IS IMPORTANT

1.It builds a strong bond amongst mother and father and children: Positive parenting strategies help create a nurturing and supportive surroundings for kids to thrive in. This fosters a strong bond among mother and father and childrenleading to a greater great and satisfying relationship.

2.It encourages first-rate conduct: Positive parenting makes a speciality of reinforcing exquisite conduct in kids in area of punishing terrible conduct. This approach lets in kids broaden powerful arrogance, strength of mind, and emotional law capabilities.

3.It teaches vital lifestyles skills: Positive parenting allows youngsters research important existence abilities which includes hassle-solving, powerful verbal exchange, and choice-making.

four.It reduces terrible behavior: By emphasizing incredible reinforcement and communication, powerful parenting techniques can reduce negative behavior in youngsters together with aggression, defiance, and disobedience.

5. It supports healthy infant improvement: Positive parenting can guide healthy little one development through way of promoting emotional well-being, social competence, and educational fulfillment.

Overall, exceptional parenting is vital because it enables mother and father create a nurturing and supportive surroundings for his or her children to thrive in, even as furthermore schooling them vital life capabilities and fostering a brilliant self-picture.

HOW POSITIVE PARENTING DIFFERS FROM TRADITIONAL DISCIPLINE METHODS

Focus on notable reinforcement: Positive parenting emphasizes high first-rate reinforcement for pinnacle behavior, in desire to punishment for horrific behavior. This manner that dad and mom hobby on profitable and praising their children after they behave nicely, in choice to the usage of punishment to accurate their behavior.

Open conversation: Positive parenting consists of open and honest communication between mother and father and youngsters. Parents use active listening skills to understand their kid's views, and encourage their youngsters to precise their emotions and evaluations.

Collaborative hassle-fixing: Positive parenting emphasizes collaborative hassle-solving, wherein mother and father artwork with their children to locate answers to problems. This approach allows kids make bigger trouble-solving skills and teaches them to take duty for his or her actions.

Natural consequences: Positive parenting uses herbal effects to train youngsters the effects in their actions. For instance, if a toddler refuses to put on a coat on a chilly day, they may experience cold and have a look at the importance of wearing suitable clothing.

Focus on building a positive relationship: Positive parenting emphasizes building a pleasant dating among mother and father and children. This approach that dad and mom reputation on growing a nurturing and supportive surroundings, in preference to in reality implementing regulations and difficulty.

Overall, brilliant parenting differs from traditional area techniques thru focusing on exquisite reinforcement, open conversation, collaborative problem-fixing, natural results, and constructing a high top notch relationship amongst mother and father and kids. By the usage of the ones strategies, mother and father can help their children amplify essential lifestyles competencies and a high-quality self-picture, at the equal time as fostering a strong and healthy courting with them.

UNDERSTANDING CHILDS BEHAVIOUR

Understanding child conduct is a important element of effective parenting. Children's behavior can variety counting on their age, developmental degree, character, and environment. Here are some key standards to keep in thoughts at the same time as looking for to apprehend infant conduct:

1. Developmental degrees: Children undergo severa developmental levels which could affect their behavior. For instance, toddlers are identified for their hobby and choice to discover, at the equal time as teenagers may be

more vulnerable to riot and risk-taking behavior.

2.Temperament: Children have special temperaments, that would have an impact on how they reply to their surroundings. Some kids may be evidently greater introverted or shy, even as others may be more outgoing and adventurous.

three.Emotions: Children experience a sizeable form of feelings, that could have an effect on their behavior. Young kids may additionally have problem expressing their feelings, which can result in frustration and tantrums.

four.Environmental factors: Children's behavior also can be brought on by using way of the use of their environment, together with their home life, college, and community. For example, a child who's exposed to violence or trauma also can display off competitive behavior.

5.Communication: Effective communique is crucial for facts toddler conduct. Parents need to actively listen to their youngsters and inspire them to particular their feelings and mind. This can assist parents better apprehend their little one's behavior and cope with any underlying problems.

By information those elements, mother and father can better apprehend their toddler's conduct and reply in a notable and powerful way. Positive parenting strategies, which incorporates fantastic reinforcement, open conversation, and collaborative trouble-solving, can assist parents pork up best conduct and educate their youngsters essential existence skills.

DEVELOPMENTAL STAGES OF CHILDREN

Children undergo numerous developmental degrees as they develop and mature. Understanding the ones stages can help parents anticipate their infant's conduct, tailor their parenting approach to their toddler's goals, and sell wholesome development. Here are some of the vital problem developmental degrees of kids:

1.Infancy: Infancy is the degree from start to 12 months. During this degree, infants growth their motor competencies, cognitive abilties, and social-emotional abilities. They learn how to pass slowly, stroll, and speak, and increase attachments to their caregivers.

2.Toddlerhood: Toddlerhood is the degree from 1 to 3 years vintage. Toddlers preserve to enlarge their motor abilities, language, and social-emotional skills. They end up greater impartial, curious, and exploratory, but also may be susceptible to tantrums and separation tension.

three.Preschool: Preschool is the extent from 3 to five years vintage. During this stage, kids extend their language and cognitive talents, and begin to extend their social talents. They may also attend preschool or kindergarten and learn how to have interaction with considered one of a type youngsters.

four.Middle youngsters: Middle early life is the diploma from 6 to eleven years antique. Children retain to develop their language, cognitive, and social abilities. They may also begin to boom a sense of identity and vanity, and come to be more unbiased.

five. Adolescence: Adolescence is the degree from 12 to 18 years vintage. Adolescents revel in huge bodily, emotional, and social adjustments. They broaden more complex cognitive talents, establish their private identification, and form relationships with friends and romantic partners.

Each developmental level offers specific worrying situations and opportunities for parents. Positive parenting techniques, together with placing easy and steady limits, the usage of terrific reinforcement, and promoting open communication, can help mother and father assist their little one's healthy development at every diploma.

Chapter 16: Common Behavioral Challenges In Each Stage

Each developmental degree offers particular stressful situations for dad and mom in phrases of little one behavior. Here are some commonplace behavioral stressful situations that mother and father might also moreover additionally face in every stage:

1. Infancy: In infancy, not unusual behavioral demanding situations can also additionally include crying, feeding troubles, and problem sleeping via the night time time.

2. Toddlerhood: In toddlerhood, commonplace behavioral demanding situations can also encompass tantrums, separation tension, and defiance. Toddlers are also recognized for exploring their surroundings and can have interaction in behaviors which might be unstable or disruptive.

3.Preschool: In preschool, common behavioral traumatic conditions may embody problem sharing, aggression closer to pals, and defiance within the direction of authority figures.

four.Middle adolescence: In middle early life, not unusual behavioral demanding conditions can also additionally encompass peer pressure, bullying, and educational strain. Children may also warfare with vanity troubles and the desire to in form in with their buddies.

five.Adolescence: In children, common behavioral traumatic situations can also encompass upward push up, danger-taking behavior, and emotional volatility. Adolescents are also navigating the complexities of identity formation and putting in place their independence from their parents.

Parents can use high-quality parenting techniques to deal with the ones behavioral stressful conditions and sell exquisite behavior of their kids. For instance, using amazing reinforcement, placing clear and steady limits, and selling open verbal exchange can help mother and father assist excessive high-quality behavior, address horrific behavior, and foster a healthful determine-toddler courting.

THE ROLE OF EMOTIONS IN BEHAVIOR

Emotions play a critical function in shaping conduct, particularly in kids. Children experience a considerable sort of feelings, together with pride, anger, worry, unhappiness, and frustration, that would impact their conduct in certainly one of a kind techniques. Here are a few strategies wherein feelings can effect behavior:

1.Behavioral triggers: Emotions can cause effective behaviors in youngsters. For instance, a toddler who feels irritated can also emerge as irritable and throw a tantrum.

2.Communication: Emotions can be a shape of communique. Children who lack the verbal capabilities to specific their emotions might also additionally act out via their behavior. For example, a infant who is feeling worrying may additionally hold close to their discern or refuse to move to high school.

three.Social interactions: Emotions play a massive function in social interactions. Children who're able to recognize and reply because it ought to be to the feelings of others are more likely to extend immoderate first-rate relationships with friends.

four. Developmental milestones: Emotions are an vital part of children's social-emotional development. Learning to regulate feelings, specific emotions because it need to be, and empathize with others are crucial developmental milestones.

5. Coping skills: Emotions can also effect a baby's coping skills. Children who're able to manipulate their emotions in a healthy manner are better ready to address disturbing situations and stressors.

As parents, it is critical to understand the placement of emotions in shaping behavior and help youngsters make bigger healthy emotional regulation talents. This can include education kids to perceive and express their emotions, modeling healthy coping skills, and providing a safe and supportive environment in which kids experience snug sharing their emotions. By fostering emotional intelligence in children, mother and father can assist them come to be properly-adjusted and resilient adults.

POSITIVE REINFORCEMENT TECHNIQUES

Positive reinforcement is a key detail of notable parenting, and involves worthwhile extraordinary behavior to inspire it to be repeated. Here are some high satisfactory reinforcement strategies that mother and father can use to sell exceptional behavior in their youngsters:

1.Praise: Praising a child for his or her high-quality behavior is a clean but effective shape of excessive excellent reinforcement. For instance, pronouncing "Great task!" or "I'm happy with you!" when a toddler follows a rule or demonstrates a notable conduct can encourage them to hold doing so.

2.Rewards: Offering rewards for terrific behavior additionally can be a form of brilliant reinforcement. This can be as clean as giving a sticker or small toy for finishing a mission, or as complicated as installing place a rewards chart in which a infant earns points or tokens for notable conduct that may be traded in for large rewards.

3.Attention: Attention additionally can be a powerful form of satisfactory reinforcement, specifically for extra younger kids. Giving a infant interest when they show off outstanding behavior can encourage them to hold doing so. For instance, giving a toddler a hug or immoderate-5 after they percentage a toy with a sibling can encourage them to hold sharing within the future.

four.Modeling: Modeling excessive wonderful behavior also can be a form of brilliant reinforcement. When parents show off high-quality behavior themselves, children are much more likely to comply with in form. For instance, while dad and mom use polite language and show admire to others, children are much more likely to do the identical.

five.Natural consequences: Allowing herbal effects to rise up additionally can be a shape of exquisite reinforcement. For instance, if a infant takes genuine care of their toys, they will be much more likely to final longer and offer greater amusement. This can strengthen the wonderful conduct of searching after one's belongings.

By using top notch reinforcement techniques, mother and father can inspire tremendous conduct of their kids with out resorting to punishment or horrible reinforcement. Positive reinforcement allows kids extend vanity, self-confidence, and exceptional attitudes closer to themselves and others.

DEFINITION OF POSITIVE REINFORCEMENT

Positive reinforcement is a form of operant conditioning in which a suitable behavior is bolstered through the addition of a reward or first-rate quit end result. When a behavior is located through using a tremendous final results, which encompass reward, hobby, or a praise, the conduct is much more likely to be repeated within the future. Positive reinforcement is a powerful tool for promoting effective conduct and analyzing new abilities, and is a key issue of remarkable parenting techniques. By offering exquisite reinforcement for correct behaviors, dad and mom can inspire their kids to amplify notable conduct and behaviors, and beef up their decide-little one dating.

EXAMPLES OF POSITIVE REINFORCEMENT TECHNIQUES

Positive reinforcement techniques are used to inspire fine behaviors in youngsters by manner of supplying a reward or exquisite impact for that behavior. Here are some examples of superb reinforcement strategies that dad and mom can use:

1.Verbal reward: This includes praising the kid with phrases for exquisite conduct, which include "Great gadget!" or "Well finished!"

2.Rewards: Rewards can be given for first rate behavior, collectively with stickers, treats, or small toys.

three.Privileges: Privileges which consist of extra display time, deciding on a family interest, or staying up past due can be given as a reward for terrific conduct.

four.Attention: Giving hobby to extremely good conduct can aid it. For instance, a figure may additionally furthermore deliver a toddler attention for playing well with a sibling.

five. Positive feedback: This entails giving the kid unique remarks about what they did nicely and why it grow to be specific, along with "I favored how you used type words along side your pal."

6. Natural effects: Allowing herbal effects to stand up additionally may be a form of first-rate reinforcement. For instance, if a toddler locations their toys away after playing with them, they'll be more likely in an effort to find out them with out difficulty the subsequent time they need to play.

It's vital to hold in mind that particular youngsters also can reply otherwise to unique varieties of reinforcement, so it can take a few trial and mistakes to locate what works first rate for each toddler. By the use of superb reinforcement techniques constantly, parents can assist their kids expand superb behaviors and conduct, and create a extra top notch and supportive own family surroundings.

www.ingramcontent.com/pod-product-compliance
Lightning Source LLC
Chambersburg PA
CBHW071445080526
44587CB00014B/1998